COMMON COR

MATH 3

WORKBOOK

MW01132252

OPERATIONS AND ALGEBRAIC THINKING

NAME: DATE:

1. Anthony delivers 12 milk boxes 4 times a week. How many milk boxes did he deliver in a week?

   A. 16 milk boxes
   B. boxes
   C. box

2. Which multiplication facts match this array?

   A. 3 × 4 and 4 ×
   B. 4 × 5 and 5
   C. 2 × 6 an
   D. 3 × 2 a

16 flowers and puts an equal wers in each any flowers does each vase?

   B. 12
   D. 4   3.OA.A.2

4. Eighte
   cam
   3 □
   s

can be used to tal number of ure?

4 + 4 =
4 + 3

OPERATIONS AND ALGEBRAIC THINKING

NAME: DATE:

6. Edward had 5 boxes of pens. Each box had 15 pens in How many pen

   B. 75 pens
   C. 20 pens
   D. 10 pens

7. and 12 crickets for dinner. Which equation can we use to find the total number of crickets the frog ate?

   A. 11 + 8 + 12 = c
   B. 11 × 8 × 12 = c
   C. 11 + 8 − 12 = c
   D. 11 × 8 + 12 = c   3.OA.A.3

9, 36 cards are dealt equally to 6 players. ach player get?

   B. 42 cards
   D. 6 cards   3.OA.A.3

prepaze

www.prepaze.com

Author: Ace Academic Publishing

Ace Academic Publishing is a leading supplemental educational workbook publisher for grades K-12. At Ace Academic Publishing, we realize the importance of imparting analytical and critical thinking skills during the early ages of childhood and hence our books include materials that require multiple levels of analysis and encourage the students to think outside the box.

The materials for our books are written by award winning teachers with several years of teaching experience. All our books are aligned with the state standards and are widely used by many schools throughout the country.

Prepaze is a sister company of Ace Academic Publishing. Intrigued by the unending possibilities of the internet and its role in education, Prepaze was created to spread the knowledge and learning across all corners of the world through an online platform. We equip ourselves with state-of-the-art technologies so that knowledge reaches the students through the quickest and the most effective channels.

For inquiries and bulk orders, contact Ace Academic Publishing at the following address:

Ace Academic Publishing
3736 Fallon Road #403
Dublin CA 94568
www.aceacademicpublishing.com

Ace Academic Publishing
ACHIEVING EXCELLENCE TOGETHER

ISBN:978-1-949383-27-0

INTRODUCTION

3

About the Book

The contents of this book includes multiple chapters and units covering all the required Common Core Standards for this grade level. Similar to a standardized exam, you can find questions of all types, including multiple choice, fill-in-the-blank, true or false, matching and free response questions. These carefully written questions aim to help students reason abstractly and quantitatively using various models, strategies, and problem-solving techniques. The detailed answer explanations in the back of the book help the students understand the topics and gain confidence in solving similar problems.

For the Parents

This workbook includes practice questions and tests that cover all the required Common Core Standards for the grade level. The book is comprised of multiple tests for each topic so that your child can have an abundant amount of tests on the same topic. The workbook is divided into chapters and units so that you can choose the topics that you want your child needs to focus on. The detailed answer explanations in the back will teach your child the right methods to solve the problems for all types of questions, including the free-response questions. After completing the tests on all the chapters, your child can take any Common Core standardized exam with confidence and can excel in it.

For additional online practice, sign up for a free account at
www.aceacademicprep.com.

For the Teachers

All questions and tests included in this workbook are based on the Common Core State Standards and includes a clear label of each standard name. You can assign your students tests on a particular unit in each chapter, and can also assign a chapter review test. The book also includes two final exams which you can use towards the end of the school year to review all the topics that were covered. This workbook will help your students overcome any deficiencies in their understanding of critical concepts and will also help you identify the specific topics that your students may require additional practice. These grade-appropriate, yet challenging, questions will help your students learn to strategically use appropriate tools and excel in Common Core standardized exams.

For additional online practice, sign up for a free account at
www.aceacademicprep.com.

www.prepaze.com

Other books from Ace Academic Publishing

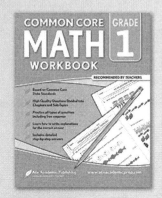

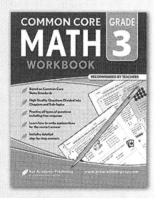
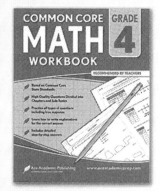

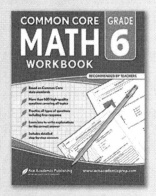
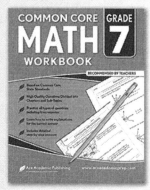
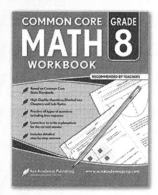

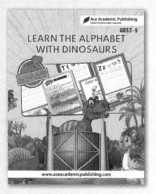

Ace Academic Publishing
ACHIEVING EXCELLENCE TOGETHER

TABLE OF CONTENTS

Operations & Algebraic Thinking

Number & Operations in Base Ten

Number & Operations - Fractions

Measurement & Data

Geometry

Comprehensive Assessment 1

Comprehensive Assessment 2

Answers and Explanations

OPERATIONS & ALGEBRAIC THINKING

www.prepaze.com

OPERATIONS AND ALGEBRAIC THINKING

GROUPING

1. Which addition equation can be used to count the total number of apples in this picture?

A. $3+3+3=n$

B. $4+4+3=n$

C. $3+4+3=n$

D. $4+4+4=n$

3.OA.A.1

2. A day on Earth is equal to 24 hours long. A day on the dwarf planet Haumea is about 4 hours long. How many Haumea days are equal to 3 Earth days?

A. 18

B. 16

C. 14

D. 12

3.OA.A.2

3. Jing makes breakfast for his brothers. He makes 12 pancakes. If each of the brothers gets 4 pancakes, how many plates should he get out?

A. 8

B. 16

C. 3

D. 4

3.OA.A.2

4. There are 20 bikes in the parking lot. If they are divided into 4 groups, how many bikes are there in each group?

A. 80 bikes

B. 16 bikes

C. 24 bikes

D. 5 bikes

3.OA.A.3

5. What is product of 3×4?

A. 10   **B.** 9

C. 12   **D.** 14

3.OA.A.1

prepaze

OPERATIONS AND ALGEBRAIC THINKING

GROUPING

6. Edward had 5 boxes of pens. Each box had 15 pens in it. How many pens did Edward have in total?

     A. 3 pens

     B. 75 pens

     C. 20 pens

     D. 10 pens

3.OA.A.3

7. Today, a frog ate 11 crickets for breakfast, 8 crickets for lunch, and 12 crickets for dinner. Which equation can we use to find the total number of crickets the frog ate?

     A. $11 + 8 + 12 = c$

     B. $11 \times 8 \times 12 = c$

     C. $11 + 8 - 12 = c$

     D. $11 \times 8 + 12 = c$

3.OA.A.3

8. To start a card game, 36 cards are dealt equally to 6 players. How many cards does each player get?

   A. 30 cards   **B.** 42 cards   **C.** 5 cards   **D.** 6 cards

3.OA.A.3

9. Which division equation represents this picture?

   A. $5 \div 3 = 15$ **B.** $15 \div 3 = 4$ **C.** $15 \div 5 = 3$ **D.** $3 \div 3 = 1$

3.OA.A.2

OPERATIONS AND ALGEBRAIC THINKING

10. There are 5 spiders spinning webs under a porch. Each spider has 8 legs. How many legs do the spiders have all together?

A. 13 legs   **B.** 40 legs
C. 45 legs   **D.** 20 legs

3.OA.A.3

11. Jeremy has 4 boxes of pencils. Each box has 8 pencils. Which expression represents the total number of pencil Jeremy has altogether?

A. 4×4 **B.** 4×8
C. 8×8 **D.** $4 + 8$

3.OA.A.1

GROUPING

12. Taylor has 19 comic books and 23 coloring books. She places them in equal stacks on her bookshelf. Her bookshelf has 6 shelves. How many books are in each stack?

A. 7 books   **B.** 4 books   **C.** 5 books   **D.** 8 books

3.OA.A.2

13. Hampton uses the model below to write the multiplication expression 4×2.

Then he writes a related addition expression: $2 + 2 + 2 + 2$.

A. Is he correct or incorrect? _____
Explain your reasoning:

_____

_____

3.OA.A.1

prepaze

OPERATIONS AND ALGEBRAIC THINKING

GROUPING

14. Look at the following groups of objects. Write a division statement to represent the picture.

_____

(3.OA.A.2)

15. Ivy had a jar of jelly beans that weighed 56 ounces. She added 16 more ounces of jelly beans to the jar. Ivy then divided the jelly beans evenly into bags that each weighed 8 ounces. How many bags of jelly beans did Ivy make?

_____

(3.OA.A.3)

16. Anna has 91 pages left to read in her chapter book. She reads 7 pages on the first night, then plans to read 12 pages each night until she is finished. How many nights will it take Anna to finish the book?

_____

(3.OA.A.3)

OPERATIONS AND ALGEBRAIC THINKING

GROUPING

17. Cameron bought 4 packs of gum with 7 pieces in each pack. Julie bought 5 packs of gum with 5 pieces in each pack. Who bought more gum?

_____

(3.OA.A.1)

18. Jennifer is planning a birthday party. She makes 21 brownies. If she plans to give each person 3 brownies, how many people are expected at the party?

_____

(3.OA.A.2)

19. Amber is setting up cupcakes for her birthday party. She organizes the cupcakes into 2 rows with 8 cupcakes in each row. Then she decides to add another 3 rows of 8 cupcakes.

A. Draw an array to show how she organized the cupcakes.

B. How many cupcakes did Amber prepare for the party?

_____

(3.OA.A.1)

prepaze

OPERATIONS AND ALGEBRAIC THINKING

GROUPING

20. Write a word problem that uses the equation 2×8.

_____

_____

_____

_____

_____

_____

3.OA.A.1

UNIT 2: PROPERTIES OF MULTIPLICATION AND DIVISION

OPERATIONS AND ALGEBRAIC THINKING

1. Use the number line below to help you find the unknown number in this equation.

$$9 = 3 \times n.$$

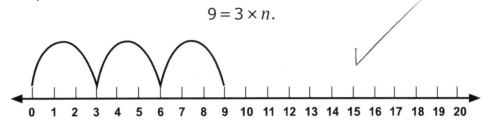

A. 5   **B.** 4   **C.** 3   **D.** 6

3.OA.A.4

2. Stephanie is setting up for an assembly. She places 24 chairs around 4 tables. Which equation can be used to determine the number of chairs at each table?

A. $24 - 4 = n$
B. $4 \times n = 24$
C. $4 + n = 24$
D. $4 \div 24 = n$

3.OA.B.6

3. Skip Which property is modeled in this equation?

$$3 \times (2 \times 8) = (3 \times 2) \times 8$$

A. Commutative Property of Multiplication
B. Associative Property of Multiplication
C. Distributive Property
D. None of the above

3.OA.B.5

4. Roger ran 15 miles on Thursday. On Saturday, he ran twice as many miles as he did on Thursday. Which equation can be used to find the number of miles Roger ran on Saturday?

A. $15 \times 2 = x$ **B.** $15 + 2 = x$
C. $15 + 17 = x$ **D.** $15 - 2 = x$

3.OA.A.4

OPERATIONS AND ALGEBRAIC THINKING

PROPERTIES OF MULTIPLICATION AND DIVISION

5. Jose placed 63 tennis balls in equal groups. There are 21 groups. Which expression represents the number of tennis balls in each group? ✓

A. $63 - 21$ **B.** $63 + 21$
C. 63×21 **D.** $63 \div 21$

3.OA.B.6

6. Which equation shows the distributive property?

A. $6 + 0 = 6$
B. $2 \times 4 = 4 \times 2$
C. $2(1 + 3) = (2 \times 1) + (2 \times 3)$
D. $6 \times 0 = 0$

3.OA.B.5

7. Hailey has 35 colored pencils. She organizes them into 7 pencil boxes. How many colored pencils are in each box?

A. There are 7 pencils in each box.
B. There are 6 pencils in each box.
C. There are 8 pencils in each box.
D. There are 5 pencils in each box.

3.OA.B.6

8. The expression $5 \times (6 + 1)$ is the same as:

A. $(5 \times 6) + (5 \times 1)$
B. $(5 + 6) + (5 + 1)$
C. $(5 + 6) \times (5 + 1)$
D. $(5 \times 6) \times (5 \times 1)$

3.OA.B.5

9. Divide the 16 stars into groups of 4. How many groups did you create?

A. 5 groups   **B.** 3 groups   **C.** 4 groups   **D.** 6 groups

3.OA.B.6

OPERATIONS AND ALGEBRAIC THINKING

10. Kelly is trying to solve a math problem that reads, "4 groups of some number is the same as 36". What equation can she use to solve this problem?

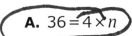 **A.** $36 = 4 \times n$ **B.** $4 + 36 = n$ **C.** $4 \times 36 = n$ **D.** $n = 4 + 4 + 4$

3.OA.A.4

12. Carly is working on solving $6 \times n = 30$. She starts with drawing 6 groups and then doesn't know what to do next. Which equation can help her solve this problem?

A. $30 \times 6 = n$
B. $n = 30 \div 6$
C. $30 = n \times 6$
D. $30 = 6 - n$

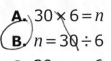

3.OA.B.5

Skip

11. Which equation shows the commutative property of multiplication?

A. $7 \times 0 = 0$
B. $4(2 + 1) = 8 + 4$
C. $9 + 1 = 1 + 9$
D. $3 \times 6 = 6 \times 3$

3.OA.B.6

13. Jose is buying fruit at the store. He buys 3 bags of apples for $4 each and 2 melons for $5 each.

A. How much money does he spend at the store? 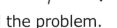 $22.⁰⁰

B. Write an equation to show how you solved the problem.

$(3 \times 4) + (2 \times 5)$
$12 + 10$
22

3.OA.A.4

14. Charlie draws apples in 6 rows of 4. How many apples did Charlie draw? _Charlie drew 24 apples_

$6 \times 4 = 24$

3.OA.B.6

prepaze

OPERATIONS AND ALGEBRAIC THINKING

15. Write a word problem using the equation $63 = 7 \times n$.

$63 \div 7 = 8$

(3.OA.A.4)

16. Fill in the blanks:

$$15 = 10 + \underline{\bigcirc} = 5 + \underline{5}$$

(3.OA.B.5)

17. Mrs. Camson writes this equation on the board:

$$49 \div 7 = n \; 7$$

Samantha says to use this equation to find the unknown number:

$$7 \times \overset{\nearrow}{n} = 49$$

Is Samantha correct? Explain your reasoning.

i moltipild 7x7 ang it =
49 thats now inew it.

(3.OA.B.6)

18. What number is missing from this equation?

$$8 \times (3 \times 9) = (8 \times \underline{\quad}) \times 3$$

(3.OA.B.5)

OPERATIONS AND ALGEBRAIC THINKING

19. Draw two arrays to represent this expression:

$$4(3+7)$$

3.OA.B.5

20. Mr. Jones posted this equation on the board:

$$n = 6 \times 8$$

Jimmy says he can count by 8 six times to solve for the unknown number. Lindsay says she can count 6 groups of 8 to solve for the unknown number. Who is correct? Explain your reasoning.

_____

_____

_____

_____

3.OA.A.4

UNIT 3: MULTIPLY AND DIVIDE WITHIN 100

OPERATIONS AND ALGEBRAIC THINKING

MULTIPLY AND DIVIDE WITHIN 100

1. Mr. Carey wrote this expression on the board: "6 fours" Which equation represents his expression?

A. $6+4=10$ **B.** $60+4=64$

C. $6\times4=24$ **D.** $6+40=46$

(3.OA.C.7)

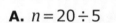

3. For each lawn that Larry mows, he earns $7. How many lawns does he need to mow to buy a video game that costs $60?

A. 8 **B.** 7

C. 9 **D.** 6

(3.OA.C.7)

5. Oliver counts 20 five-dollar bills in his pocket. Which equation can be used to determine n the total amount of money Oliver has in his pocket?

A. $n=20\div5$ **B.** $n=5\times20$

C. $20=n\times5$ **D.** $20+5=n$

(3.OA.C.7)

2. Caleb has 23 baseball cards and 18 basketball cards. He wants to divide the cards into 4 boxes equally. Which value is the best estimate of how many cards he will put into each box?

23
+ 18
41

A. 15 cards

B. 20 cards

C. 8 cards

D. 10 cards

(3.OA.D.8)

4. Which number is always a factor of a 2-digit number ending in 5?

A. 10 **B.** 2

C. 4 **D.** 5

(3.OA.D.9)

6. Kalida has 6 bags of 5 books in each bag. She gives away 12 books and receives 3 more from her teacher. Which equation represents the number of books Kalida has left?

A. $(6\times5)-(12-3)=n$ **B.** $(6+5)-(12+3)=n$

C. $(6\times5)-12+3=n$ **D.** $(6\times5)+(12-3)=n$

(3.OA.D.8)

OPERATIONS AND ALGEBRAIC THINKING

7. Leo is trying to simplify this expression: 6×8. Which expression is equivalent to 6×8?

A. $(6 \times 5) + (6 \times 4)$
B. $(6 \times 6) + (6 \times 3)$
C. $(6 \times 5) + (6 \times 3)$
D. $(6 \times 5) - (6 \times 3)$

3.OA.D.9

8. The temperature on a spring day was 75 degrees in the morning. During the afternoon, the temperature rose 4 degrees and then at night it was 68 degrees. How much did the temperature drop from the afternoon to night time?

A. 10 degrees   **B.** 12 degrees
C. 9 degrees   **D.** 11 degrees

3.OA.D.8

9. Gavin saved $8 a day for 6 days. He wants to buy new sneakers that cost $56 dollars. How many more days does Gavin have to work so he will have enough money to buy the sneakers?

A. 2 days   **B.** 1 day
C. 8 days   **D.** 4 days

3.OA.D.8

10. What is the pattern in this number sequence?

3, 6, 12, 24

A. Add 6
B. Multiply by 2
C. Add 3
D. Multiply by 3

3.OA.C.7

11. Carin is having trouble solving $48 \div 8$. She can use the multiplication fact 8×5 and then:

A. Add a group of 5   **B.** Subtract a group of 8
C. Add a group of 8   **D.** Subtract a group of 5

3.OA.D.9

prepaze

OPERATIONS AND ALGEBRAIC THINKING

MULTIPLY AND DIVIDE WITHIN 100

12. Which expression shows another way to simplify 7×6?

    A. $(7 \times 2) + (7 \times 3)$ **B.** $(7 \times 4) + (7 \times 4)$

    C. $(7 \times 3) + (7 \times 3)$ **D.** $(7 \times 2) + (7 \times 2)$

(3.OA.D.9)

13. Maggie spent $81 buying plants at the florist. Each plant costs $9. Which equation represents the number of plants Maggie bought?

    A. $81 \div 9 = 9$ **B.** $9 \times 8 = 81$

    C. $81 - 9 = 72$ **D.** $81 \div 9 = 8$

(3.OA.C.7)

14. Gerald is having trouble simplifying the expression 8×9. Which strategy can he use?

    A. 8×7 and then add one group of 7

    B. 9×9 and subtract one group of 9

    C. 9×9 and subtract one group of 8

    D. 8×8 and add one group of 9

(3.OA.D.9)

15. Sherry says any number that is divisible by 6 is also divisible by 3. Is she correct? Explain her reasoning.

_____

_____

_____

_____

(3.OA.D.9)

OPERATIONS AND ALGEBRAIC THINKING

16. Write a word problem for this equation: $(16 + 29) - 18 =$

_____

_____

_____

_____

3.OA.D.8

17. Sally sells her cookies in the amount shown below. Jane needs 65 cookies for a party.

SALLY'S COOKIES	
Boxes	**Number of Cookies**
1	8
2	16
3	24
4	32

A. How many boxes of cookies should Jane buy so she has enough for her party? _____

B. Will Sally have any cookies left over? _____

3.OA.D.8

18. Will the product of two odd numbers always result in an even or odd number? Explain your reasoning.

_____

_____

_____

_____

3.OA.D.9

prepaze

OPERATIONS AND ALGEBRAIC THINKING

MULTIPLY AND DIVIDE WITHIN 100

19. Explain how you can solve this equation using pictures, arrays or a number line.

$$36 \div 3 = n$$

3.OA.C.7

20. Clara has $65 from her birthday party. Five days later, she has $5 left. If she spent the same amount of money on lunch every day, how much did she pay for lunch? Explain how you found your answer using an equation.

_____

_____

_____

_____

3.OA.D.8

CHAPTER REVIEW ➡

OPERATIONS AND ALGEBRAIC THINKING

1. Anthony delivers 12 milk boxes 4 times a week. How many milk boxes did he deliver in a week?

A. 16 milk boxes

B. 3 milk boxes

C. 48 milk boxes

D. 8 milk boxes

3.OA.A.3

2. Which multiplication facts match this array?

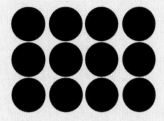

A. 3×4 and 4×3 ✓

B. 4×5 and 5×4

C. 2×6 and 6×2

D. 3×2 and 2×3

3.OA.B.5

3. Yoanna has 16 flowers and 4 vases. She puts an equal number of flowers in each vase. How many flowers does Yoanna put in each vase?

A. 20

B. 12

C. $86 \div 4 =$

D. 4 ✓

3.OA.A.2

4. Eighteen boy scouts are going camping. Each tent sleeps 3 people. How many tents should the boy scouts bring so everyone has a place to sleep?

A. 5 tents

B. 8 tents ✓

C. 3 tents

D. 6 tents

3.OA.A.4

5. Which equation can be used to determine the total number of apples in this picture?

 ✓

A. $3 + 3 + 3 =$

B. $4 + 4 + 4 =$

C. $3 + 4 + 3 =$

D. $4 + 4 + 3 =$

3.OA.A.1

OPERATIONS AND ALGEBRAIC THINKING

CHAPTER REVIEW

6. Logan works 10 hours a week. He earns $8 each hour. How much money does Logan earn in a week?

A. $75

B. $70

C. $18

D. $80

3.OA.C.7

7. Lacey bought 4 bags with 8 red apples in each bag and 3 bags with 6 green apples in each bag. How many apples did Lacey buy altogether?

A. 45 apples

B. 50 apples

C. 52 apples

D. 48 apples

3.OA.D.8

8. Karen bought 20 mangos. She gave 5 mangos to each to her friends. How many friends does Karen have?

A. 3 friends

B. 25 friends

C. 4 friends

D. 15 friends

3.OA.A.3

9. A 2-digit number that ends in zero is always divisible by:

A. 10

B. 6

C. 4

D. 3

3.OA.D.9

10. Choose the equation that shows the distributive property.

A. $6+0=6$

B. $2+4=4+2$

C. $2(7+13)=(2\times7)+(2\times13)$

D. $6\times5=5\times6$

3.OA.B.5

prepaze

OPERATIONS AND ALGEBRAIC THINKING

11. Mr. Porter needs 56 cups for his party. The cups come in packs of 8. How many packs should Mr. Porter buy for the party?

A. 7   **B.** 8
C. 6   **D.** 9

3.OA.C.7

12. What is the answer to a division problem called?

A. divisor
B. quotient
C. dividend
D. subtrahend

3.OA.A.2

13. Which model represents this equation?

$$12 \div 4 = 3$$

A.

B.

C.

D.

3.OA.B.6

14. To find the value of 8×4, which multiplication fact can be used?

A. 8×1
B. 8×3
C. 8×4
D. 8×2

3.OA.D.9

15. Irene did 8 push-ups everyday until she reached 48 push-ups. Which division equation would help us find out how many days Irene did push-ups? (*d* stands for days)

A. $\frac{48}{4} = d$ **B.** $\frac{8}{48} = d$ **C.** $\frac{48}{8} = d$ **D.** $\frac{48}{d} = 8$

3.OA.A.3

prepaze

OPERATIONS AND ALGEBRAIC THINKING

CHAPTER REVIEW

16. Choose the equation that shows the associative property of multiplication.

A. $11+(7+3)=(11+7)+3$
B. $2+4=4+2$
C. $2\times(8\times5)=(2\times8)\times5$
D. $12\times0=0$

3.OA.B.5

17. A number that is divisible by 4 will always be divisible by:

A. 6
B. 2
C. 5
D. 3

3.OA.D.9

18. At the fair, Casey bought 9 chocolate bars for his family. How much money did he spend? The following chart shows the unit price for candies.

CANDY	PRICE
Chocolate Bar	$2
S'more	$4
Cheesecake	$7
Tray of cookies	$9

A. $16　　B. $20　　C. $18　　D. $17

3.OA.A.1

19. Aiden is sorting his video games. He has 56 video games to organize onto 8 shelves. He thinks of this as a division problem $56\div8=n$. What other equation can be used to determine the number of video games Aiden will put on each shelf?

A. $n=56\times8$
B. $56-8=n$
C. $56=n\times8$
D. $8+n=56$

3.OA.A.4

OPERATIONS AND ALGEBRAIC THINKING

20. Janice decides to make bracelets to give her friends. She has 24 pieces of blue string, 6 pieces of yellow string, and 30 pieces of red string. She uses 10 strings for each bracelet. How many friends will receive a bracelet?

A. 60   **B.** 10   **C.** 30   **D.** 6

3.OA.A.2

EXTRA PRACTICE

prepaze

OPERATIONS AND ALGEBRAIC THINKING

EXTRA PRACTICE

1. Ariel has 32 shells and puts an equal number of shells into 4 bags. How many shells does Ariel put into each bag?

A. 6   **B.** 16

C. 9   **D.** 8

3.OA.B.6

2. Which equation could represent this diagram?

| 7 | 7 | 7 | 7 | 7 |

A. $7 \times 7 = 35$ **B.** $35 \div 5 = 7$

C. $7 + 5 = 35$ **D.** $28 \div 7 = 4$

3.OA.A.4

3. Mrs. Jones is using 30 pieces of candy to make party favors for John's birthday. She puts 5 pieces of candy in each bag. Which equation shows the number of party favor bags Mrs. Jones uses?

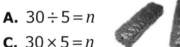

A. $30 \div 5 = n$ **B.** $30 - n = 5$

C. $30 \times 5 = n$ **D.** $5 + n = 30$

3.OA.A.4

4. Which numbers can be divided evenly into 100?

A. 3, 6 and 5   **B.** 7, 8 and 2

C. 9, 1, and 10   **D.** 4, 5 and 2

3.OA.C.7

5. Eduardo makes an array using 2 rows of 6 tiles. He adds 4 more rows to the array. Which multiplication sentence does Eduardo's array show?

A. $2 \times 10 = 20$ **B.** $6 \times 6 = 36$

C. $2 \times 4 = 8$ **D.** $4 \times 6 = 24$

3.OA.B.5

prepaze   **www.prepaze.com**

OPERATIONS AND ALGEBRAIC THINKING

6. Sammy made $15 babysitting on Friday and $28 babysitting on Saturday. On Sunday, she bought lunch for $14. How much money does Sammy have left?

A. $31   **B.** $29   **C.** $30   **D.** $28

3.OA.D.8

7. Ashley bakes 3 trays of 10 muffins. She eats 2 for breakfast. Then she gives an equal number of muffins to 7 of her friends. How many muffins does Ashley share with each friend?

A. 4   **B.** 13   **C.** 30   **D.** 22

3.OA.A.2

8. Gary drew 8 legs on each spider and drew 48 legs. How many spiders did Gary draw? Choose the equation needed to solve this problem.

A. $48 = n \times 7$ **B.** $48 = 8 \times n$ **C.** $8 + n = 48$ **D.** $48 = 8 \div n$

3.OA.B.6

9. Kaitlin must read a 50-page book. She reads 14 pages on Sunday and the reads the same number of pages each night for the next 4 days. How many pages does she read each night? Choose the equation to solve this problem

A. $p = (50 + 14) \div 4$ **B.** $p = 50 - 14 - 4$

C. $(50 - 14) \div 4 = p$ **D.** $(50 \div 4) - 14 = p$

3.OA.D.8

prepaze

OPERATIONS AND ALGEBRAIC THINKING

10. Carlos has 5 stacks of 8 books and Maria has 6 stacks of 7 books. Who has more books? Explain your reasoning.

3.OA.C.7

11. Mr. Harding bought 8 pizzas for a pizza party. Half of the pizzas have pepperoni on them. If there are 8 slices in each pizza, how many pizza slices have pepperoni? Explain how you found your answer using an equation.

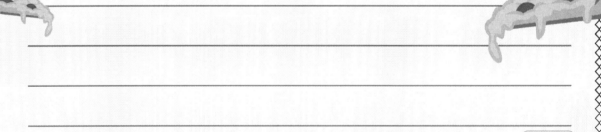

3.OA.D.8

12. Arthur can either work 6 hours a week for $9 an hour at the coffee shop or he can work for 7 hours a week for $8 an hour at the bookstore. Where will he make the most money in one week, the bookstore or the coffee shop?

3.OA.C.7

OPERATIONS AND ALGEBRAIC THINKING

13. Kayla is making bracelets for her 5 friends. She uses 9 beads to make each bracelet.

  A. How many beads will she need to make the bracelets for her friends?

  _____

  B. Draw a picture show how you found the answer:

  C. Write an equation that solves this problem:

3.OA.A.1

14. Will the product of an even number and an odd number be an even or odd number? Explain your reasoning.

_____

_____

_____

_____

3.OA.D.9

prepaze

OPERATIONS AND ALGEBRAIC THINKING

15. Ivy had a jar of jelly beans that weighed 56 ounces. She added 16 more ounces of jelly beans to the jar. Ivy then divided the jelly beans evenly into bags that each weighed 8 ounces. How many bags of jelly beans did Ivy make?

_____

(3.OA.A.3)

16. It costs $125 for 10 tickets to the movie theater. The price of each ticket is $9, and the cost includes a fee for lunch for the group. How much does the lunch cost? Explain how you found your answer using an equation.

_____

_____

_____

(3.OA.D.8)

17. Georgina needs new notebooks for school. She spends $30 and received $2 in change. If Georgina purchased 7 notebooks and each notebook cost the same amount, how much money did each notebook cost? Explain your thinking.

_____

_____

_____

_____

(3.OA.A.4)

OPERATIONS AND ALGEBRAIC THINKING

18. Use this number line to answer the questions below:

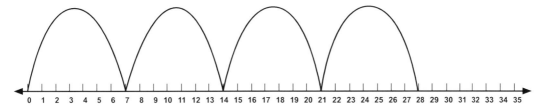

A. Write a multiplication equation for this number line: _____

B. Write a division equation for this number line: _____

C. What number is the quotient? _____

D. Which number is the dividend? _____

E. Which number is the divisor? _____

(3.OA.B.6)

19. Write a word problem that represents the equation 2×8.

_____

_____

_____

_____

(3.OA.A.1)

20. Terrance has roll of 15 crackers. He eats 3 crackers. Then he gives an equal amount to his friends, Anne and Paul. How many crackers do Anne and Paul each receive?

_____

(3.OA.A.2)

prepaze

NUMBER & OPERATIONS IN BASE TEN

prepaze

www.prepaze.com

NUMBER & OPERATIONS IN BASE TEN

1. Mrs. Carr made a fruit salad using 112 banana slices. Which number represents the number of banana slices she used rounded to the nearest 10?

   A. 112
   B. 110 ✓
   C. 100
   D. 200

3.NBT.A.1

2. Janelle made a fruit salad using 217 orange slices. Which number represents the number of orange slices she used rounded to the nearest 100?

   A. 300
   B. 100
   C. 220 ✓
   D. 200

3.NBT.A.1

Confeusd

3. Andy is counting his stickers. He has about 180 stickers when he rounds the number to the nearest ten. Which number could represent the actual number of stickers Andy has?

   A. 175   B. 186
   C. 192   D. 172

3.NBT.A.1

4. A farmer harvests between 400 and 500 strawberries. The number of strawberries rounded to the nearest hundred is closer to 500. Which number could represent the actual number of strawberries?

   A. 425   B. 505
   C. 461   D. 550

3.NBT.A.1

5. A pecan tree produces between 200 and 300 acorns. The number of acorns rounded to the nearest ten is 200. Which number could represent the actual number of acorns?

   A. 198   B. 295   C. 204   D. 290

Confeusd

3.NBT.A.1

prepaze

PLACE VALUE ROUNDING

6. James is collecting coins. He already has 43 and adds 29 to his collection. Which number shows the number of coins he has rounded to the nearest ten?

A. 40   **B.** 90
C. 100   **D.** 70

3.NBT.A.1

7. Alyssa has 17 balls. Which number represents the number of balls Alyssa has rounded to the nearest 100?

A. 100   **B.** 0
C. 50   **D.** 20

3.NBT.A.1

8. The toy store has 125 bikes. Which number represents the number of bikes the toy store has rounded to the nearest 10?

A. 200
B. 120
C. 130
D. 100

3.NBT.A.1

9. The toy store has close to 700 teddy bears. This estimate is found by rounding the actual number to the nearest 10. Which number represents the actual number of teddy bears in the toy store?

A. 704
B. 685
C. 798
D. 649

3.NBT.A.1

10. The toy store has close to 1,000 packs of cards. This estimate is found by rounding the actual number to the nearest 100. Which number represents the actual number of cards in the toy store?

A. 930   **B.** 1,031
C. 1,195   **D.** 949

3.NBT.A.1

NUMBER & OPERATIONS IN BASE TEN

11. Mr. Williams has 39 students in his class. Mrs. Johnson has 28 students in her class. Mr. Jackson has 21 students in his class. Which number represents the estimate of the number of students in all 3 classrooms rounded to the nearest ten?

A. 100   **B.** 70
C. 50   **D.** 90

3.NBT.A.1

12. Caren has 1,025 pieces of candy. How many pieces of candy does she have rounded to the nearest 100?

A. 1,100
B. 1,000
C. 1,030
D. 1,125

3.NBT.A.1

13. You collect stickers and have 311 star stickers. Rounded to the nearest ten, about how many star stickers do you have?

_____

3.NBT.A.1

14. You collect stickers and have 284 animal stickers. Rounded to the nearest ten, about how many animal stickers do you have?

_____

3.NBT.A.1

15. You collect stickers and have 3,995 superhero stickers. Rounded to the nearest hundred, about how many superhero stickers do you have?

_____

3.NBT.A.1

NUMBER & OPERATIONS IN BASE TEN

PLACE VALUE ROUNDING

16. You collect stickers and have 74 smiley face stickers. Rounded to the nearest hundred, about how many smiley face stickers do you have?

_____

3.NBT.A.1

17. Isaiah has 10 fewer stickers than Sarah. Sarah rounds the number of stickers she has to the nearest ten and has about 30 stickers. Which number could represent the number of stickers Isaiah has?

_____

3.NBT.A.1

18. While driving, you see 121 pickup trucks. Rounded to the nearest ten, about how many pickup trucks did you see?

_____

3.NBT.A.1

19. While driving, you see 206 cars. Rounded to the nearest ten, about how many cars did you see?

_____

3.NBT.A.1

20. While driving, you see 185 minivans. Rounded to the nearest hundred, about how many minivans do you see?

_____

3.NBT.A.1

UNIT 2: ADD AND SUBTRACT WITHIN 1000

prepaze

NUMBER & OPERATIONS IN BASE TEN

1. Which strategy could describe the first step in determining the value of this expression?

$$876 - 528$$

    A. Subtract 6 ones from 8 ones.

    B. Regroup 7 tens and 6 ones as 6 tens and 16 ones.

    C. Subtract 2 tens from 7 tens.

    D. Regroup 7 tens and 6 ones as 76 ones.

(3.NBT.A.2)

2. Which number makes this equation true?

$$851 + 109 - 487 = \underline{\hspace{3cm}} + 145$$

    A. 422   **B.** 318   **C.** 328   **D.** 473

(3.NBT.A.2)

3. Ronaldo buys a box of candy. There are 200 pieces inside the box. He gives 50 pieces to each of his two sisters and eats 10 pieces. Which number sentence can be used to determine how many candies he has left?

    A. $200 - (50 + 50) - 10 = \underline{\hspace{2cm}}$

    B. $200 - 50 - 10 = \underline{\hspace{2cm}}$

    C. $200 + 50 + 50 + 10 = \underline{\hspace{2cm}}$

    D. $200 - (50 + 10) = \underline{\hspace{2cm}}$

(3.NBT.A.2)

prepaze

NUMBER & OPERATIONS IN BASE TEN

4. This graph shows the number of miles Mr. Wilson travels each month. How many miles does Mr. Wilson travel between June and September?

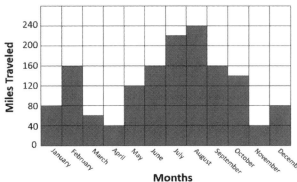

A. 460 miles   **B.** 760 miles

C. 780 miles   **D.** 320 miles

3.NBT.A.2

5. Which model represents the value of this expression?

$$1,000 - 789$$

A.

B.

C.

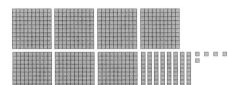

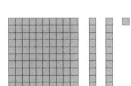

D.

3.NBT.A.2

NUMBER & OPERATIONS IN BASE TEN

6. Which statement explains why the missing value in this equation is 630?

$$950 - 630 + \underline{\hspace{3cm}} = 320 + 630$$

A. 630 is on both sides of the equation.

B. Both expressions will have a value of 950.

C. 630 is less than 950.

D. The difference between 950 and 320 is 630.

(3.NBT.A.2)

7. Which statement describes a strategy for determining the value of this expression?

$$419 - 149 - 50 + 381$$

A. Find the sum of 149 and 50, then subtract the difference of 419 and 381.

B. Find the sum of 419 and 381, then subtract the sum of 149 and 50.

C. Find the difference of 419 and 149, and add it to the sum of 50 and 381

D. Find the difference of 419 and 50, then add it to the sum of 149 and 381.

(3.NBT.A.2)

8. Which strategy describes a first step which can be used to simplify this expression?

$$546 - 205 - 195 + 234$$

A. Find the sum of 205 and 200, then add 5 more.

B. Add 46 and 34, then subtract 700 more.

C. Subtract 200 from 546, then subtract 5 more.

D. Subtract 200 from 546, then add 5 more.

(3.NBT.A.2)

prepaze

NUMBER & OPERATIONS IN BASE TEN

ADD AND SUBTRACT WITHIN 1000

9. Liam and Sophia are reading the same book. Explain how you would determine the total number of pages Liam and Sophia have read.

- The book has a total of 238 pages.
- Liam must read 111 pages to finish the book.
- Sophia must read 182 pages to finish the book.

_____

_____

_____

_____

(3.NBT.A.2)

10. Olivia writes a three-digit number in her math journal. The number she writes is 356 less than 894. She then adds 187 to the number written in her journal. What is the value of the new number?

_____

(3.NBT.A.2)

11. Which number makes this equation true?

$$109 + 315 + 287 = \underline{\hspace{1cm}} + 471$$

(3.NBT.A.2)

12. Which number makes this equation true?

$$1{,}000 - 746 + 203 = 628 - \underline{\hspace{1cm}}$$

(3.NBT.A.2)

prepaze

NUMBER & OPERATIONS IN BASE TEN

13. Ms. Tonji has 3 boxes of calculators.

- □ There are 130 calculators in the first box.
- □ There is a total of 270 calculators in the second and third boxes.
- □ There are twice as many calculators in the second box as in the third box.

a) Which box has the greatest number of calculators?

_____

b) How would you determine the number of calculators in the second and third boxes?

_____

c) What is the total number of calculators in all three boxes?

_____

3.NBT.A.2

14. Model this expression on the number line.

$$105 + 585$$

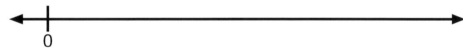

3.NBT.A.2

15. Model this expression on the number line.

$$948 - 235 + 187$$

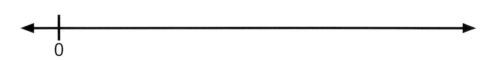

3.NBT.A.2

prepaze

NUMBER & OPERATIONS IN BASE TEN

16. This graph shows the number of miles Mr. Wilson travels each month. How many more miles does Mr. Wilson drive in August and September than in January and February?

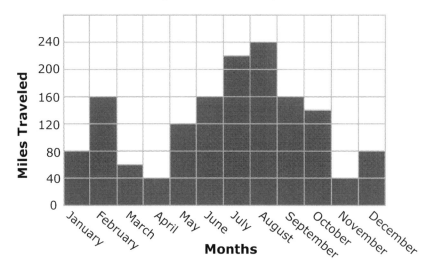

_____

3.NBT.A.2

17. What is the difference between the values of Model A and Model B?

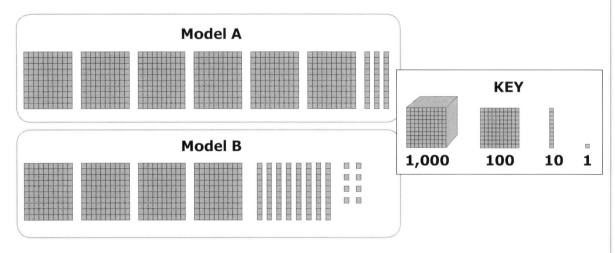

_____

3.NBT.A.2

NUMBER & OPERATIONS IN BASE TEN

18. This table shows the greatest number of travelers on 5 airplanes.

Airplane	Number of Travelers
Airbus A380	495
Airbus A320	220
Boeing 727	189
Boeing 777	451
Boeing 747	366

Two airplanes, an Airbus A320 and Boeing 727, are flown across the country and back. If all the seats on both airplanes are filled for these flights, do they carry more travelers than an Airbus A380 making the same trip? Explain your reasoning.

_____

_____

_____

_____

3.NBT.A.2

prepaze

NUMBER & OPERATIONS IN BASE TEN

ADD AND SUBTRACT WITHIN 1000

19. How would you correct the mistake made in solving this equation using the standard algorithm?

$$846$$
$$+ 139$$
$$\overline{975}$$

_____

_____

_____

_____

3.NBT.A.2

20. How would you correct the mistake made in solving this equation using the standard algorithm?

$$715$$
$$+ 686$$
$$\overline{171}$$

_____

_____

_____

_____

3.NBT.A.2

UNIT 3: MULTIPLY BY 10

NUMBER & OPERATIONS IN BASE TEN

1. What is the value of 2 tens?

A. 10

B. 20

C. 2

D. 22

3.NBT.A.3

2. Samuel says he has four $10 bills in his pocket. How much money does Samuel have?

A. $10   **B.** $4

C. $40   **D.** $30

3.NBT.A.3

3. Carly has 6 plates with 10 cookies on each plate. Which equation can be used to determine the total number of cookies Carly has?

A. $10 \times 10 =$ **B.** $6 \times 10 =$

C. $6 \times 6 =$ **D.** $6 + 10 =$

3.NBT.A.3

4. A charter bus can carry 20 passengers. How many passengers can 4 buses carry?

A. 40   **B.** 60   **C.** 80   **D.** 50

3.NBT.A.3

5. Kristian has $50 that he wants to share with 5 friends. Which equation can you use to determine how much money each friend receives?

A. $10 \times 5 = 50$ **B.** $50 - 10 = 40$

C. $10 + 5 = 13$ **D.** $50 - 5 = 45$

3.NBT.A.3

6. Tommy has 3 ten-dollar bills. Samantha has 5 ten-dollar bills. Erica has 1 ten-dollar bill. How much money do they have altogether?

A. $60   **B.** $80

C. $90   **D.** $120

3.NBT.A.3

MULTIPLY BY 10

prepaze

NUMBER & OPERATIONS IN BASE TEN

MULTIPLY BY 10

7. Joan uses place value blocks to build an array. She builds an array with 4 rows of 5 tens. Which equation represents this array?

A. $5 \times 10 = 50$

B. $4 \times 5 = 20$

C. $40 \times 10 = 400$

D. $4 \times 50 = 200$

3.NBT.A.3

8. Jerry needs paper plates for his party. He buys 6 packs of 30 plates. How many plates did Jerry buy?

A. 150 plates

B. 180 plates

C. 190 plates

D. 160 plates

3.NBT.A.3

9. Colby saved up his money and now has ten $10 bills. How much money did Colby save?

A. $100

C. $120

B. $110

D. $101

3.NBT.A.3

10. The hardware store sells nails in packs of 50. Brendan buys 6 packs of nails. Which equation can be used to find the total number of nails Brendan bought?

A. $6 + 5 \times 10 =$

C. $6 \times 5 \times 10 =$

B. $50 + 6 =$

D. $(10 + 5) \times 6 =$

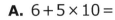

3.NBT.A.3

11. The model below represents a multiplication equation: Based on this model, which number makes this equation true?

$3 \times (? \times 10) =$

A. 10

C. 12

B. 3

D. 4

3.NBT.A.3

NUMBER & OPERATIONS IN BASE TEN

MULTIPLY BY 10

12. If there are 60 minutes in 1 hour, how many minutes are in 8 hours and 15 minutes?

- **A.** 480 minutes
- **B.** 495 minutes
- **C.** 630 minutes
- **D.** 505 minutes

3.NBT.A.3

13. Which equation can be used to solve 40×8?

- **A.** $(4 \times 10) \times 8$
- **B.** $(8 \times 10) + 4$
- **C.** $(4 + 8) \times 10$
- **D.** 100×32

3.NBT.A.3

14. A shopping bag with 8 apples weighs 170 ounces. If the empty shopping bag weighs 10 ounces, how much does each apple weigh?

- **A.** 30 ounces
- **B.** 20 ounces
- **C.** 60 ounces
- **D.** 10 ounces

3.NBT.A.3

15. Mr. Stapleton buys 9 boxes of soda. Each box has 14 cans of cherry sodas and 16 cans of regular sodas. Which equation can be used to determine how many sodas Mr. Stapleton buys?

- **A.** $(9 + 16) \times 14$
- **B.** $9 \times 16 \times 14$
- **C.** $(14 \times 9) + 16$
- **D.** $(14 + 16) \times 9$

3.NBT.A.3

16. Roger solves 30×5 by using the expression 10×15. Explain his reasoning.

_____

_____

_____

_____

3.NBT.A.3

prepaze

NUMBER & OPERATIONS IN BASE TEN

MULTIPLY BY 10

17. There are 6 seats on one row of a passenger train car.

   A. If there are 20 rows in one passenger train car, how many seats are there?

_____

   B. How many seats are on 4 passenger train cars?

_____

3.NBT.A.3

18. Peyton saves $40 a month for 7 months. He wants to buy a new scooter for $290. Does Peyton have enough money to buy the scooter? If not, how much more money is needed?.

3.NBT.A.3

19. Sawyer has 10 boxes of cookies with 4 cookies in each box.
Emily has 2 boxes of cookies that each contain 2 bags of 10 cookies.
Do Emily and Sawyer have the same number of cookies? Explain.

_____

_____

_____

_____

3.NBT.A.3

prepaze

NUMBER & OPERATIONS IN BASE TEN

20. Lauren bought 5 packs of trading cards. Each pack has 37 regular cards and 3 special cards. She lost 14 cards. How many cards does Lauren have left? Explain the steps you used to solve:

_____

_____

_____

_____

3.NBT.A.3

MULTIPLY BY 10

CHAPTER REVIEW

prepaze

NUMBER & OPERATIONS IN BASE TEN

1. Which response could describe a first step for evaluating this expression?

$$59 + 182 + 31 + 208$$

A. Add 5 tens, 8 tens, and 3 tens, then regroup as hundreds.

B. Add 9 ones, 2 ones, 1 one and 8 ones, then regroup as tens.

C. Add 5 tens, 1 hundred, 3 tens, and 2 hundreds, then regroup as thousands.

D. Add 1 hundred and 2 hundreds, then regroup as thousands.

(3.NBT.A.2)

2. There are 123 pages in Emily's math book, and 276 pages in her social studies book. What is the total number of pages in both books rounded to the nearest hundred?

A. 399   **B.** 400   **C.** 410   **D.** 390

(3.NBT.A.1)

3. Which response could describe a first step for evaluating this expression?

$$840 - 164 - 259$$

A. Start by subtracting 164 from 259. Subtract 4 ones from 9 ones.

B. Start by adding 164 and 259. Subtract 3 hundreds from 8 hundreds in 840.

C. Start with 840 − 164. Regroup 4 tens as 14 ones.

D. Start with 840 − 164. Regroup 4 tens as 3 tens and 10 ones.

(3.NBT.A.3)

NUMBER & OPERATIONS IN BASE TEN

CHAPTER REVIEW

4. Jacki uses the standard algorithm to find the value of this expression.

$$1,000 - 609 - 238$$

Which response shows her first step?

A. $1,000 + 238$ **B.** $238 - 609$
C. $1,000 - 609$ **D.** $609 - 1,000$

3.NBT.A.3

5. Anna has 23 pencils. Her mom buys her 18 more. About how many pencils does she have rounded to the nearest ten?

A. 30   **B.** 35   **C.** 40   **D.** 45

3.NBT.A.2

6. What is the total distance around Murray Park?

Murray Park

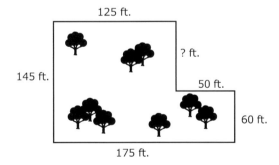

125 ft.
? ft.
145 ft.
50 ft.
60 ft.
175 ft.

A. 565 ft.   **B.** 640 ft.   **C.** 445 ft.   **D.** 1,045 ft.

3.NBT.A.2

NUMBER & OPERATIONS IN BASE TEN

7. What are the two missing values in this illustration?

Lindale Park

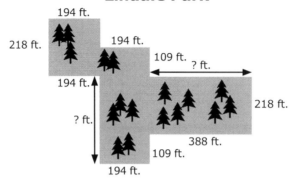

194 ft.

218 ft.   194 ft.

109 ft.   ? ft.

194 ft.

? ft.   218 ft.

388 ft.

109 ft.

194 ft.

A. 109 ft. and 218 ft.   **B.** 388 ft. and 218 ft.
C. 388 ft. and 327 ft.   **D.** 327 ft. and 582 ft.

3.NBT.A.1

8. Mark made $346 last month. He made $567 this month. About how much money did he make rounded to the nearest hundred?

A. $800   **B.** $830
C. $1,000   **D.** $900

3.NBT.A.3

9. Jennie has 1,756 cows in her farm. Lisa has 3,963 cows in her farm. Rounded to the nearest hundred, about how many cows do they have in all?

A. 4,600   **B.** 5,800
C. 4,700   **D.** 5,000

3.NBT.A.2

10. Sam worked for 54 hours this month. He worked for 27 hours last month Rounded to the nearest ten, about how many hours did he work?

A. 90   **B.** 70   **C.** 80   **D.** 100

3.NBT.A.3

NUMBER & OPERATIONS IN BASE TEN

11. There are 568 students at the school in 9th grade. They are 426 students at the school in 10th grade. Rounded to the nearest hundred, about how many students are in 9th and 10th grade combined?

    A. 900   **B.** 990   **C.** 1,100   **D.** 1,000

(3.NBT.A.2)

12. The students at Storey Elementary want to raise $900 to buy new computers. They raise $225 from a fundraiser. A company agrees to give the students twice the amount they raise to help them buy the computers. How much more money must the students at Storey Elementary raise to buy the computers?

(3.NBT.A.1)

13. Joy collects marbles. She has 839 marbles currently. As a gift, she received 357 more from her friends. Rounded to the nearest hundred, about how many marbles are in her collection now?

(3.NBT.A.3)

14. Bobby received 371 candy bars for Halloween. His brother receives 133 candy bars for Halloween. Rounded to the nearest ten, about how many candy bars did they receive?

(3.NBT.A.2)

prepaze

NUMBER & OPERATIONS IN BASE TEN

15. Jay has 733 toys in his room. Dean has 284 toys in his room. Crush has 823 toys in his room. Rounded to the nearest hundred, about how many toys do the boys have in their rooms altogether?

_____

3.NBT.A.2

16. Irene received 499 flowers for her birthday. Rounded to the nearest ten, about how many flowers did she receive?

_____

3.NBT.A.1

17. Thomas has $423. His father gives him $125, and he spends $275 on a new game system. Write a number sentence to represent the amount of money Thomas has left.

_____

3.NBT.A.1

18. What expression is modeled on this number line?

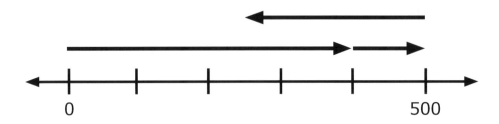

_____

3.NBT.A.3

prep☺ze

NUMBER & OPERATIONS IN BASE TEN

19. What expression is modeled on this number line?

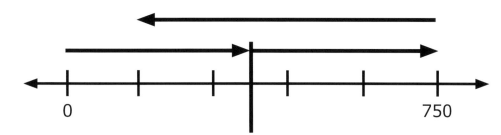

CHAPTER REVIEW

3.NBT.A.1

20. What expression is modeled on this number line?

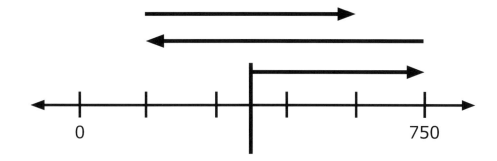

3.NBT.A.3

EXTRA PRACTICE

prepaze

NUMBER & OPERATIONS IN BASE TEN

1. Mr. Johnson has 15 books on each shelf. If there are 4 shelves, which expression can be used to determine the number of books Mr. Johnson has altogether?

   A. 30×2 **B.** 15×2
   C. 30×4 **D.** 15×15

3.NBT.A.2

2. Sarah spends 45 minutes each day watching tv. Which expression represents the number of minutes Sarah spends watching tv for 6 days?

   A. 90×2 **B.** 45×45
   C. 90×3 **D.** 60×6

3.NBT.A.1

3. April spends 20 minutes on her homework for each subject. On Monday and Tuesday evening, April has homework in mathematics, science, and social studies. How much time does April spend on her homework on Monday and Tuesday?

   A. 120 minutes   **B.** 60 minutes
   C. 40 minutes   **D.** 100 minutes

3.NBT.A.3

4. There are 5 boxes of construction paper in the art room. Two boxes each have 30 sheets of construction paper, and the remaining boxes each have 40 sheets of construction paper. How many sheets of construction paper are in the boxes?

   A. 180 sheets   **B.** 150 sheets
   C. 200 sheets   **D.** 350 sheets

3.NBT.A.3

5. Mr. Nilson buys 7 boxes of markers for her students' art project. 3 of the boxes have 20 markers, and the remaining boxes have 10 markers. How many markers does Mr. Nilson buy?

   A. 30 markers   **B.** 100 markers
   C. 140 markers   **D.** 70 markers

3.NBT.A.1

NUMBER & OPERATIONS IN BASE TEN

6. Claire reads 34 pages of her book on Monday, 79 pages on Tuesday and 54 pages on Wednesday. The book has 200 pages. How many more pages does Claire have to read to finish the book?

A. 33 pages   **B.** 157 pages
C. 167 pages   **D.** 367 pages

3.NBT.A.3

7. Tamir collects coins. His coin collection has pennies, quarters and half dollars. Tamir has $2.50 in pennies, $10 in quarters, and $4 in half dollars. How many coins does he have altogether?

A. 1,650   **B.** 354
C. 264   **D.** 298

3.NBT.A.1

8. Which expression is equivalent to 4×30?

A. 2×60 **B.** $4 + 30$
C. 8×60 **D.** $2 + 60$

3.NBT.A.1

9. Larena recites this poem to remember the number of days in each month throughout the year:

"Thirty days are in September, April, June and November"
There are 365 days in a year. Which expression represents the number of days in the remaining 8 months of the year?

A. $365 - (30 \times 8)$ **B.** $365 \times (30 \times 4)$
C. $365 - (30 \times 4)$ **D.** $365 + (30 \times 8)$

3.NBT.A.2

10. Jaren buys 6 packages of hot dogs. Each package contains 10 hot dogs. He serves the hot dogs at a party where 48 people attend. How many hot dogs does Jaren have left after the party?

3.NBT.A.2

NUMBER & OPERATIONS IN BASE TEN

11. There are 12 packages of balloons left in the store. Each package has 30 balloons. Mark purchases half of the packages. How many balloons does Mark purchase?

_____

(3.NBT.A.1)

12. Haley's class sells 50 tickets to the school play. Each ticket costs $7. Haley's class has a goal of earning $420 from ticket sales. How much more money do they need to make?

_____

(3.NBT.A.3)

13. Harry has 7 boxes of colored pencils. Each box has 15 colored pencils. He estimates he has about 140 pencils. Do you agree with Harry? Explain your reasoning.

_____

_____

_____

(3.NBT.A.2)

14. Which of these two expressions has the greater value? Explain your reasoning.

$$(50 \times 8) \qquad (80 \times 5)$$

_____

_____

(3.NBT.A.1)

NUMBER & OPERATIONS IN BASE TEN

15. Elliot exercises for the same amount of time each day. He exercises for 176 minutes six days each week. Approximately how much time does Elliot spend exercising each day?

_____

3.NBT.A.3

16. Write 3 expressions equivalent to the one shown:

$$60 \times 2$$

_____

_____

3.NBT.A.2

17. Landon's dog weighs approximately 20 pounds. Houston's dog weighs exactly 18 pounds. Do you know whose dog weighs the most? Explain your reasoning.

_____

_____

_____

3.N BT.A.1

18. Oscar and his 5 friends each have $20. Each of them receive an additional $6 from their parents. How much money do they have altogether?

_____

3.NBT.A.3

prepaze

NUMBER & OPERATIONS IN BASE TEN

19. This table shows 5 numbers rounded to the nearest hundred. Which number is incorrectly rounded to the nearest hundred? Explain your reasoning.

STARTING NUMBER	NUMBER ROUNDED TO THE NEAREST HUNDRED
4,095	4,100
5,581	5,600
9,971	9,900
948	900
3,297	3,300

_____

_____

_____

3.NBT.A.1

20. Using the standard algorithm, how would you describe the process of adding these numbers?

$$307 + 154$$

_____

_____

_____

3.NBT.A.2

NUMBER & OPERATIONS FRACTIONS

www.prepaze.com

NUMBER & OPERATIONS – FRACTIONS

1. Which number line shows $\frac{1}{3}$?

A.
B. ✓
C. (circled)
D.

(3.NF.A.2.A)

2. The triangles below represent one whole. What fractional part of the model is NOT shaded?

A. $\frac{3}{5}$ ✓   B. $\frac{2}{5}$

C. $\frac{3}{6}$ D. $\frac{2}{6}$

(3.NF.A.1)

3. What is the length of this paperclip?

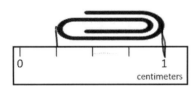

A. 1 centimeter   B. $\frac{3}{4}$ of a centimeter ✓

C. $\frac{3}{5}$ of a centimeter   D. $\frac{4}{5}$ of a centimeter

(3.NF.A.2.B)

4. Julie has 9 crayons. 4 of her crayons are red. What fractional part of Julie's crayons are NOT red?

A. $\frac{4}{9}$ B. $\frac{3}{9}$ C. $\frac{5}{9}$ (circled) ✓   D. $\frac{9}{4}$

(3.NF.A.1)

5. Which fraction describes the length shown on this number line?

A. $\frac{2}{3}$ of a unit
B. $\frac{1}{2}$ of a unit ✓ (circled)
C. $\frac{1}{3}$ of a unit
D. $\frac{1}{1}$ of a unit

(3.NF.A.2.A)

NUMBER & OPERATIONS – FRACTIONS

6. How long is this insect?

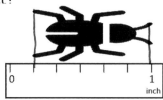

A. 1 inch   **B.** $\frac{5}{6}$ of an inch ✓   **C.** $\frac{1}{6}$ of an inch   **D.** $\frac{6}{7}$ of an inch

3.NF.A.2.B

7. Which fraction represents the length shown on this number line?

A. $\frac{1}{6}$ ✓   **B.** $\frac{1}{7}$ **C.** $\frac{3}{6}$ **D.** $\frac{3}{7}$

3.NF.A.2.A

8. Nancy has a piece of fabric that is 8 feet long. She cuts the fabric into pieces that are each 2 feet long. What fraction of the fabric does one piece represent?

A. $\frac{2}{6}$ **B.** $\frac{1}{8}$ **C.** $\frac{8}{2}$ **D.** $\frac{1}{4}$

3.NF.A.1

9. The point on this number line represents the number of miles between Lorena and Valencia's houses. Which fraction represents this distance?

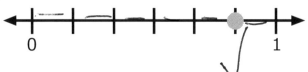

A. $\frac{6}{7}$ of a mile   **B.** $\frac{6}{1}$ of a mile   **C.** $\frac{5}{6}$ of a mile   **D.** $\frac{5}{7}$ of a mile

3.NF.A.2.B

NUMBER & OPERATIONS – FRACTIONS

10. The model below represents one whole. What is another way to name the shaded part?

A. $\frac{3}{5}$

B. $\frac{6}{3}$

C. $\frac{1}{2}$

D. $\frac{3}{3}$

3.NF.A.1

11. Martin wants to represent the fraction $\frac{1}{8}$ on a number line. Which number line is divided into 8 equal parts?

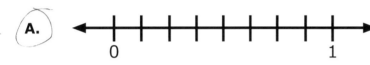

A.

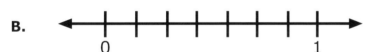

B.

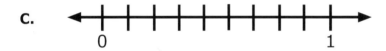

C.

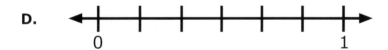

D.

3.NF.A.2.A

12. Sandra bakes a cake and shares it equally with her 4 sisters. What fractional part of the cake will each person receive?

A. $\frac{1}{4}$

B. $\frac{2}{4}$

C. $\frac{1}{5}$

D. $\frac{5}{1}$

3.NF.A.1

prepaze

NUMBER & OPERATIONS – FRACTIONS

UNDERSTANDING FRACTIONS

13. Shanell walks from the grocery store to Isaiah's house. How far does Shanell walk?

Grocery Store

Isaiah's House

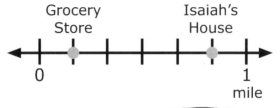

0   1 mile

A. $\frac{5}{6}$ of a mile

B. $\frac{4}{6}$ of a mile

C. $\frac{4}{7}$ of a mile

D. $\frac{1}{6}$ of a mile

3.NF.A.2.B

14. What fraction represents the length shown on this number line?

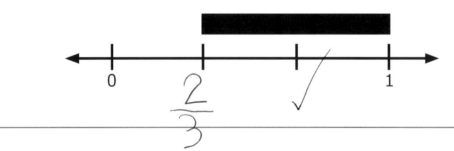

0   1

$\frac{2}{3}$ ✓

3.NF.A.2.B

15. Which fraction is represented by Point X? It Represents one half.

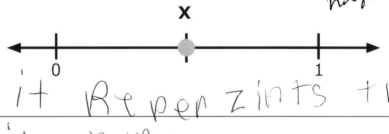

X

0   1

it Reperzints the mitle number

middle

3.NF.A.2.A

NUMBER & OPERATIONS – FRACTIONS

16. Charlie shares this pie with his 5 friends for his birthday.

 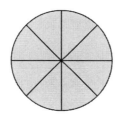 

A. Did he cut the pie into sixths? _____

B. Divide this model into sixths.

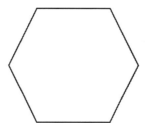

3.NF.A.1

17. Bethany believes the length of this ribbon is 1 inch. Do you agree with Bethany? Explain your thinking.

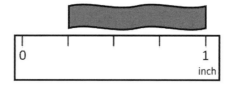

_____

_____

_____

_____

3.NF.A.2.B

prepaze

NUMBER & OPERATIONS – FRACTIONS

UNDERSTANDING FRACTIONS

18. Where is the fraction $\frac{1}{3}$ located on this number line? Explain your thinking.

_____

_____

_____

_____

3.NF.A.2.A

19. Which fraction modeled on the two rectangles below is larger? Explain your reasoning.

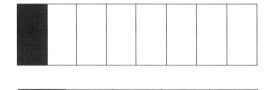

_____

_____

_____

_____

3.NF.A.1

NUMBER & OPERATIONS – FRACTIONS

20. Nathan draws two number lines. He decides the value of Point A and Point B are the same. Do you agree with Nathan? Explain your thinking.

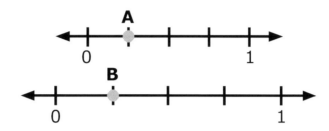

_____

_____

_____

_____

3.NF.A.2.A

UNDERSTANDING FRACTIONS

UNIT 2:   EQUIVALENT FRACTIONS

prepaze

NAME: .... DATE: ....

NUMBER & OPERATIONS – FRACTIONS

EQUIVALENT FRACTIONS

1. Which two fractions have the same value?

   A. $\frac{3}{6}$ and $\frac{3}{8}$ **B.** $\frac{1}{3}$ and $\frac{2}{3}$ **C.** $\frac{3}{6}$ and $\frac{1}{2}$ **D.** $\frac{1}{4}$ and $\frac{1}{3}$

3.NF.A.3.B

2. Umar needs this piece of ribbon to wrap a gift. Which fraction is equivalent to the length of this ribbon?

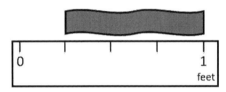

   A. $\frac{3}{6}$ of a foot   **B.** $\frac{7}{8}$ of a foot   **C.** $\frac{6}{8}$ of a foot   **D.** $\frac{2}{3}$ of a foot

3.NF.A.3.A

3. Which fraction has the same value as $\frac{1}{2}$?

   A. $\frac{2}{4}$ **B.** $\frac{6}{3}$ **C.** $\frac{5}{6}$ **D.** $\frac{3}{3}$

3.NF.A.3.B

4. Lara makes this quilt with her grandmother. Which fraction represents the part of the quilt made of white tiles?

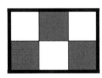

   A. $\frac{3}{3}$ **B.** $\frac{4}{8}$

   C. $\frac{1}{3}$ **D.** $\frac{4}{6}$

3.NF.A.3.A

5. Which fraction is equivalent to the shaded portion of this model?

   A. $\frac{3}{4}$ **B.** $\frac{1}{8}$

   C. $\frac{2}{3}$ **D.** $\frac{1}{2}$

3.NF.A.3.B

prep∂ze   **www.prepaze.com**

NUMBER & OPERATIONS – FRACTIONS

6. This number line shows the distance between different places in Noah's town. Which fraction is equivalent to the distance between the park and the mall?

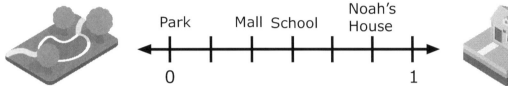

A. $\frac{3}{7}$ of a unit   **B.** $\frac{2}{5}$ of a unit   **C.** $\frac{1}{3}$ of a unit   **D.** $\frac{1}{6}$ of a unit

3.NF.A.3.A

7. Isadore represents a fraction using this model. Which fraction represents the part of the model that is shaded?

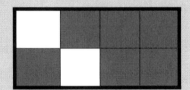

A. $\frac{3}{4}$ **B.** $\frac{6}{2}$

C. $\frac{2}{8}$ **D.** $\frac{6}{6}$

3.NF.A.3.B

8. This number line shows the distance between different places in Sarah's town. Which fraction is equivalent to the distance between the Sarah's house and the school?

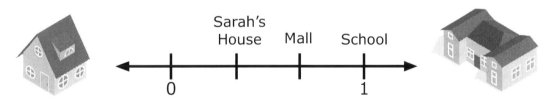

A. $\frac{4}{6}$ of a unit   **B.** $\frac{1}{3}$ of a unit   **C.** $\frac{2}{4}$ of a unit   **D.** $\frac{6}{8}$ of a unit

3.NF.A.3.A

prepaze

NUMBER & OPERATIONS – FRACTIONS

EQUIVALENT FRACTIONS

9. Which fraction is equivalent to the shaded part of Model A?

Model A

A. $\frac{1}{4}$ B. $\frac{2}{6}$

C. $\frac{1}{3}$ D. $\frac{3}{4}$

3.NF.A.3.B

10. Which fraction is equivalent to Point A?

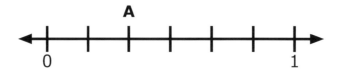

A. $\frac{3}{6}$ B. $\frac{2}{4}$ C. $\frac{1}{3}$ D. $\frac{3}{7}$

3.NF.A.3.A

11. Which model shows a fraction equivalent to $\frac{2}{3}$?

   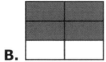   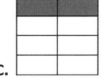

A.   B.   C.   D.

3.NF.A.3.B

12. Write one fraction equivalent to value of Point A.

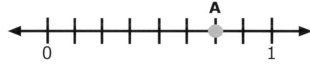

3.NF.A.3.A

prepaze   www.prepaze.com

NUMBER & OPERATIONS – FRACTIONS

13. What fraction is equivalent to the one shown in this model?

_____

3.NF.A.3.B

14. Write one fraction equivalent to value of Point A.

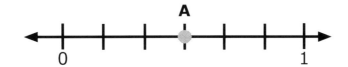

_____

3.NF.A.3.A

15. How can you use these number lines to prove whether $\frac{1}{4}$ and $\frac{2}{8}$ are equivalent? Explain your reasoning.

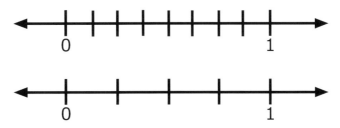

_____

_____

3.NF.A.3.B

prepaze

NUMBER & OPERATIONS – FRACTIONS

EQUIVALENT FRACTIONS

16. Yolanda says the lengths shown on Number Lines A and B are equivalent. Do you agree with Yolanda? Explain your reasoning.

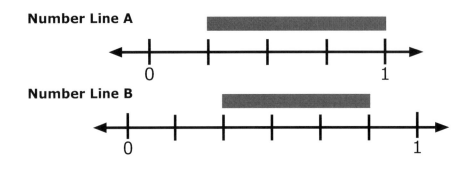

_____

_____

_____

3.NF.A.3.A

17. How would you shade these rectangles to show $\frac{1}{3}$ and $\frac{2}{6}$ are equivalent fractions? Shade each rectangle to represent these fractions.

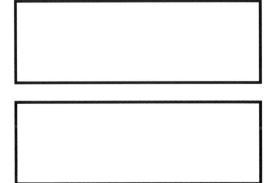

3.NF.A.3.B

NUMBER & OPERATIONS – FRACTIONS

18. Penny says the lengths shown on Number Lines A and B are equivalent. Do you agree with Penny? Explain your reasoning.

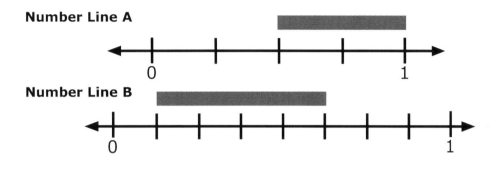

Number Line A

0   1

Number Line B

0   1

_____

_____

_____

_____

(3.NF.A.3.A)

19. Use the circles below to show $\frac{4}{5}$ and $\frac{8}{10}$. How do these fractions compare to each other?

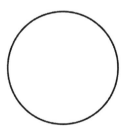 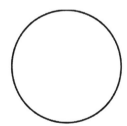

_____

_____

(3.NF.A.3.B)

prepaze

NUMBER & OPERATIONS – FRACTIONS

EQUIVALENT FRACTIONS

20. This number line shows the distance Riley walks to school.

This number line shows the distance John walks to school.

How does the distance Riley walks to school compare to the distance John walks to school?

_____

_____

_____

3.NF.A.3.A

UNIT 3:   COMPARE FRACTIONS

NUMBER & OPERATIONS – FRACTIONS

1. William is comparing these 3 numbers. Which statement correctly describes the relationship between these numbers?

$$\frac{4}{4} \qquad 1 \qquad \frac{5}{6}$$

A. The fraction $\frac{4}{4}$ is less than $\frac{5}{6}$.

B. One whole is less than $\frac{4}{4}$.

C. The fraction $\frac{4}{4}$ is equivalent to 1.

D. One whole is less than $\frac{5}{6}$.

3.NF.A.3.C

2. Which inequality is true?

A. $\frac{1}{3} > \frac{1}{2}$ **B.** $\frac{5}{6} < \frac{6}{8}$ **C.** $\frac{2}{4} < \frac{5}{8}$ **D.** $\frac{2}{3} < \frac{3}{6}$

3.NF.A.3.D

3. Terrell is comparing these numbers. Which statement correctly describes the relationship between these numbers?

$$\frac{3}{3} \qquad \frac{2}{1} \qquad \frac{8}{8} \qquad \frac{6}{1}$$

A. The fraction $\frac{3}{3}$ is less than $\frac{2}{1}$.

B. The fraction $\frac{6}{1}$ is less than $\frac{8}{8}$.

C. One whole is equivalent to $\frac{2}{1}$.

D. One whole is equivalent to $\frac{6}{1}$.

3.NF.A.3.C

4. Which inequality is true?

A. $\frac{1}{6} < \frac{1}{8}$ **B.** $\frac{3}{4} > \frac{3}{6}$ **C.** $\frac{4}{8} > \frac{1}{2}$ **D.** $\frac{2}{3} < \frac{5}{8}$

3.NF.A.3.D

prepaze

NUMBER & OPERATIONS – FRACTIONS

COMPARE FRACTIONS

5. Which fraction is equivalent to 8?

    A. $\frac{8}{0}$ **B.** $\frac{1}{8}$

    C. $\frac{8}{1}$ **D.** $\frac{8}{8}$

3.NF.A.3.C

6. Peter lives between $\frac{1}{4}$ and $\frac{3}{4}$ miles from school. Which fraction could represent the distance Peter lives from school?

    A. $\frac{1}{2}$ **B.** $\frac{1}{6}$

    C. $\frac{3}{3}$ **D.** $\frac{1}{8}$

3.NF.A.3.D

7. Which fraction is the same as 9?

    A. $\frac{9}{9}$ **B.** $\frac{9}{0}$

    C. $\frac{9}{1}$ **D.** $\frac{1}{9}$

3.NF.A.3.D

8. Which statement is true?

    A. $\frac{12}{2}=\frac{6}{1}$ **B.** $\frac{4}{5}=\frac{8}{9}$

    C. $\frac{3}{3}=\frac{4}{12}$ **D.** $\frac{6}{5}=\frac{5}{4}$

3.NF.A.3.D

9. Which fraction will complete this equation?

$$\frac{5}{6} = \text{_____}$$

    A. $\frac{6}{5}$ **B.** $\frac{10}{12}$ **C.** $\frac{1}{2}$ **D.** $\frac{8}{9}$

3.NF.A.3.D

10. Porsha uses this model to represent $\frac{8}{8}$. Draw a model to represent $\frac{8}{1}$.

3.NF.A.3.C

NUMBER & OPERATIONS – FRACTIONS

11. In a third grade survey, $\frac{2}{6}$ of the students said they enjoy playing basketball and $\frac{4}{6}$ of them said they enjoy playing Soccer. Which sport is enjoyed the most?

_____

3.NF.A.3.C

12. Model A and Model B refer to the same whole. Write an inequality to compare the fraction represented by Model A to the fraction represented by Model B.

Model A   **Model B**

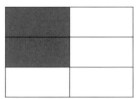 

_____

3.NF.A.3.D

13. The distance between Sam's house and school is $\frac{3}{4}$ mile. This distance between school and the park is $\frac{3}{6}$ mile. Write an inequality to compare these distances.

_____

3.NF.A.3.D

prepaze

14. Write a fraction to represent the value of Point A.

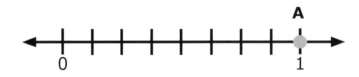

3.NF.A.3.C

15. The distance between the zoo and the park is $\frac{4}{6}$ mile. The distance between the park and city hall is $\frac{4}{8}$ mile. Write an inequality to compare these distances.

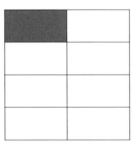
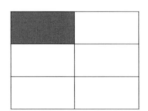

3.NF.A.3.D

16. Model A and Model B refer to the same whole. Write an inequality to compare the fraction represented by Model A to the fraction represented by Model B.

Model A

Model B

3.NF.A.3.D

NUMBER & OPERATIONS – FRACTIONS

COMPARE FRACTIONS

17. Eric creates these 4 models to represent fractions. Which model is equivalent to $\frac{4}{4}$?

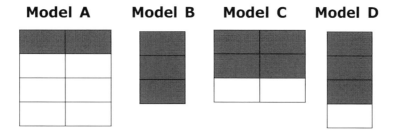

Model A   Model B   Model C   Model D

3.NF.A.3.C

18. Jason believes $\frac{1}{5}$ and $\frac{1}{4}$ are equivalent because they have the same numerator. Do you agree with Jason? Explain your reasoning.

_____

_____

_____

3.NF.A.3.D

19. Breanna believes $\frac{7}{8}$ and $\frac{5}{8}$ are equivalent because they have the same denominator. Do you agree with Breanna? Explain your reasoning.

_____

_____

_____

_____

3.NF.A.3.D

prepaze

NUMBER & OPERATIONS – FRACTIONS

COMPARE FRACTIONS

20. Eric creates these 4 models to represent fractions. Which model is equivalent to $\frac{3}{3}$?

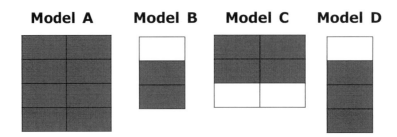

3.NF.A.3.C

NUMBER & OPERATIONS – FRACTIONS

1. Which number line models a fraction created by dividing one whole into 6 equal parts?

A.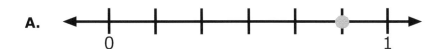

B.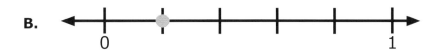

C.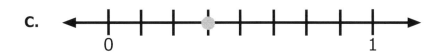

D.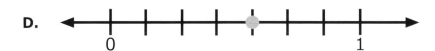

3.NF.A.2.A

2. Marco drew a circle and cut the circle into 8 equal-sized pieces. Then he colored in 3 pieces. What fractional part of the circle did Marco color?

A. $\frac{3}{8}$ **B.** $\frac{3}{3}$ **C.** $\frac{8}{3}$ **D.** $\frac{8}{8}$

3.NF.A.2.B

3. Carla makes a model to represent the days of the week. She goes to the gym on Mondays and Wednesdays. What fraction represents Carla's gym days each week?

A. $\frac{2}{8}$ **B.** $\frac{2}{7}$ **C.** $\frac{7}{2}$ **D.** $\frac{2}{5}$

3.NF.A.1

prepaze

NUMBER & OPERATIONS – FRACTIONS

CHAPTER REVIEW

4. Which fraction describes the distance between Points A and B?

A. $\frac{2}{3}$ of a unit   B. $\frac{2}{1}$ of a unit

C. $\frac{1}{3}$ of a unit   D. $\frac{2}{4}$ of a unit

3.NF.A.3.A

5. Which fraction describes the length shown on this number line?

A. $\frac{2}{3}$ of a unit   B. $\frac{1}{2}$ of a unit

C. $\frac{1}{3}$ of a unit   D. $\frac{1}{1}$ of a unit

3.NF.A.2.A

6. Heather ate one-fifth of her birthday cake. What fraction of the birthday cake did Heather not eat?

A. $\frac{4}{5}$ B. $\frac{1}{5}$ C. $\frac{1}{4}$ D. $\frac{2}{5}$

3.NF.A.3.B

NUMBER & OPERATIONS – FRACTIONS

7. Which statement describes the relationship between Number Line A and Number Line B?

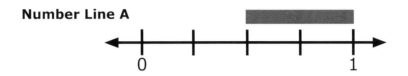

A. The fraction modeled on Number Line A is the same as the fraction modeled on Number Line B.

B. The fraction modeled on Number Line A is $\frac{3}{5}$ and the fraction modeled on Number Line B is $\frac{5}{9}$.

C. The fraction modeled on Number Line A is $\frac{2}{4}$ and the fraction modeled on Number Line B is $\frac{5}{8}$.

D. The fraction modeled on Number Line A is less than the fraction modeled on Number Line B.

3.NF.A.1

8. Which fraction is modeled on this number line?

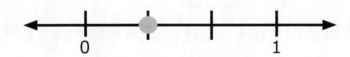

A. $\frac{2}{4}$ **B.** $\frac{1}{2}$ **C.** $\frac{1}{4}$ **D.** $\frac{1}{3}$

3.NF.A.3.B

prepaze

NUMBER & OPERATIONS – FRACTIONS

9. Which fractions are NOT equivalent?

    A. $\frac{1}{3}$ and $\frac{3}{9}$ **B.** $\frac{3}{6}$ and $\frac{5}{8}$ **C.** $\frac{2}{5}$ and $\frac{4}{10}$ **D.** $\frac{1}{2}$ and $\frac{3}{6}$

3.NF.A.3.C

10. Which statement describes this model?

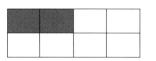 =

    Model A   Model B

    A. $\frac{2}{8}=\frac{1}{4}$ **B.** $\frac{2}{8}>\frac{1}{4}$ **C.** $\frac{2}{8}<\frac{1}{4}$ **D.** $\frac{2}{8}=\frac{1}{3}$

3.NF.A.2.A

11. Which fraction represents the length shown on this number line?

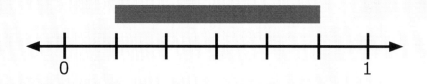

3.NF.A.1

12. Write two fractions which can be used to describe this model?

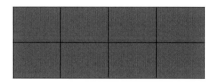

3.NF.A.3.B

NUMBER & OPERATIONS – FRACTIONS

CHAPTER REVIEW

13. Write a number sentence to describe this model.

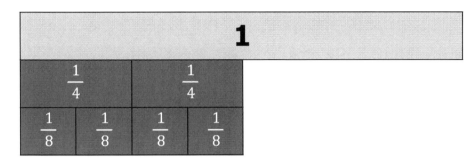

3.NF.A.3.A

14. Holden walks from the park to his house. How far does Holden walk?

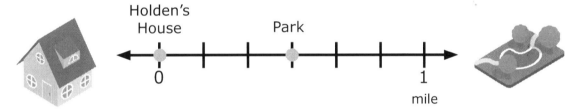

_____ of a mile

3.NF.A.2.B

15. Which fraction is represented by Point X on this number line?

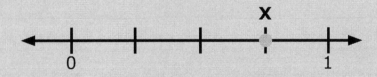

3.NF.A.3.A

prepaze

16. Write a number sentence to describe this model.

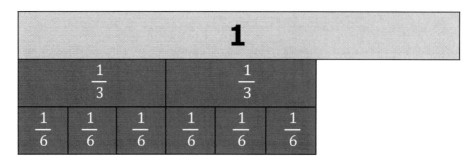

_____

3.NF.A.3.D

17. Write two fractions equivalent to Point A.

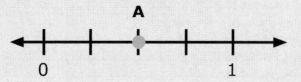

_____   _____

3.NF.A.1

18. DeWayne says that each part of this number line has a size of $\frac{1}{6}$. Do you agree with DeWayne? Explain your reasoning.

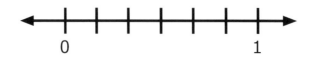

_____

_____

_____

3.NF.A.3.D

NUMBER & OPERATIONS – FRACTIONS

19. What fraction is being modeled on this number line?

0   1

3.NF.A.3.C

20. Ysleta says $\frac{3}{4}$ is equivalent to $\frac{6}{8}$. Draw a model to prove Ysleta's statement is true.

3.NF.A.2.B

EXTRA PRACTICE

prepaze

NAME: .... DATE: ....

NUMBER & OPERATIONS – FRACTIONS

EXTRA PRACTICE

1. Which fraction is modeled on this number line?

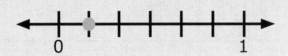

A. $\frac{1}{1}$ **B.** $\frac{1}{5}$ **C.** $\frac{1}{6}$ **D.** $\frac{1}{7}$

3.NF.A.3.D

2. The model below represents one whole. What fractional part is shaded?

A. $\frac{1}{3}$ **B.** $\frac{1}{2}$

C. $\frac{2}{3}$ **D.** $\frac{3}{3}$

3.NF.A.3.D

3. Arianna shades in part of this picture. Which fraction represents the part of the picture Arianna shaded?

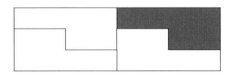

A. $\frac{1}{3}$ **B.** $\frac{3}{12}$

C. $\frac{2}{6}$ **D.** $\frac{2}{5}$

3.NF.A.2.A

4. A number line has endpoints of 0 and 1, with 5 equal parts between the endpoints. Which fraction represents each part?

A. $\frac{5}{5}$ **B.** $\frac{6}{6}$ **C.** $\frac{1}{6}$ **D.** $\frac{1}{5}$

3.NF.A.1

5. Which strategy can be used to generate an equivalent fraction?

A. Add $\frac{1}{1}$ to the fraction   **B.** Multiply the fraction by $\frac{2}{2}$

C. Multiply the fraction by $\frac{1}{2}$ **D.** Add $\frac{2}{2}$ to the fraction

3.NF.A.3.D

NUMBER & OPERATIONS – FRACTIONS

6. The model below represents one whole. What fractional part is shaded?

A. $\dfrac{3}{3}$ **B.** $\dfrac{2}{5}$ **C.** $\dfrac{3}{6}$ **D.** $\dfrac{1}{6}$

3.NF.A.3.A

7. Which strategy can be used to generate a fraction that is equivalent to ⁶/₈.

A. $\dfrac{6}{8} \times \dfrac{1}{3}$ **B.** $\dfrac{6}{8} + \dfrac{3}{3}$ **C.** $\dfrac{6}{8} + \dfrac{1}{1}$ **D.** $\dfrac{6}{8} \times \dfrac{3}{3}$

3.NF.A.2.A

8. Which fraction is equivalent to 4?

A. $\dfrac{4}{4}$ **B.** $\dfrac{4}{1}$ **C.** $\dfrac{1}{4}$ **D.** $\dfrac{8}{4}$

3.NF.A.3.C

9. Which fraction represents the length of the bar shown on this number line?

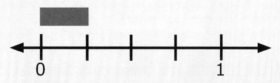

A. $\dfrac{1}{4}$ **B.** $\dfrac{1}{5}$ **C.** $\dfrac{2}{5}$ **D.** $\dfrac{2}{4}$

3.NF.A.3.B

prepaze

NUMBER & OPERATIONS – FRACTIONS

EXTRA PRACTICE

10. Mona colored $\frac{2}{8}$ of this area model. Which fraction is equivalent to $\frac{2}{8}$?

    A. $\frac{2}{6}$ **B.** $\frac{1}{3}$ **C.** $\frac{3}{9}$ **D.** $\frac{1}{4}$

3.NF.A.3.C

11. Which two fractions name the location of the point on this number line?

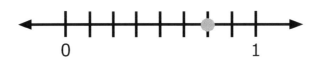

    A. $\frac{6}{2}, \frac{8}{4}$ **B.** $\frac{7}{9}, \frac{14}{18}$ **C.** $\frac{3}{4}, \frac{9}{12}$ **D.** $\frac{2}{3}, \frac{7}{9}$

3.NF.A.2.B

12. Laron wants to represent the fraction $\frac{3}{8}$ on a number line. Which number line is divided into 8 equal parts?

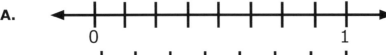

3.NF.A.3.C

prepaze

NUMBER & OPERATIONS – FRACTIONS

13. Which fraction names the location of the point on this number line?

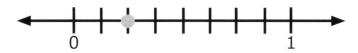

A. $\frac{1}{4}$ **B.** $\frac{2}{9}$ **C.** $\frac{3}{9}$ **D.** $\frac{4}{10}$

(3.NF.A.3.B)

14. Jonathan draws these two fraction models. Each model has the same whole. Which statement describes these models?

Model A   **Model B**

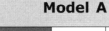

A. The shaded part of Model A is equivalent to the shaded part of Model B.

B. The shaded part of Model A and Model B are greater than 1.

C. The shaded part of Model A is less than the shaded part of Model B.

D. The shaded part of Model A is greater than the shaded part of Model B.

(3.NF.A.2.B)

15. Aliyah draws these two fraction models. Each model has the same whole. Which statement describes these models?

Model A   **Model B**

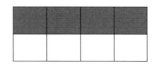

A. The shaded part of Model A is less than the shaded part of Model B.

B. The shaded part of Model A and Model B are greater than 1.

C. The shaded parts in Model A and Model B are the same.

D. The shaded part of Model A is greater than the shaded part of Model B.

(3.NF.A.2.B)

NAME: ....   DATE: ....

NUMBER & OPERATIONS – FRACTIONS

16. Which model is equivalent to $\frac{4}{4}$?

A.

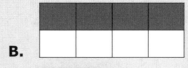

B.

C.

D.

3.NF.A.3.B

17. The distance between Barack's house and the park is $\frac{3}{5}$ miles. The distance between the park and Barack's school is $\frac{4}{5}$ miles. Which statement correctly describes these distances?

A. The distance between Barack's house and the park is the greater distance.

B. The distance between Barack's house and the park is the same as the distance between the park and Barack's school.

C. The distance between Barack's house and the park is 1 mile more than the distance between the park and Barack's school.

D. The distance between the park and Barack's school is the greater distance.

3.NF.A.3.A

18. Which statement correctly describes a relationship between two fractions in this table?

$$\frac{3}{5} \qquad \frac{3}{4} \qquad \frac{3}{3} \qquad \frac{3}{10} \qquad \frac{3}{1}$$

A. $\frac{3}{10} > \frac{3}{1}$ **B.** $\frac{3}{5} > \frac{3}{4}$ **C.** $\frac{3}{4} > \frac{3}{1}$ **D.** $\frac{3}{1} > \frac{3}{3}$

3.NF.A.2.A

prepaze

NUMBER & OPERATIONS – FRACTIONS

19. Which statement correctly describes a relationship between two fractions in this table?

$$\frac{1}{6} \qquad \frac{3}{6} \qquad \frac{4}{6} \qquad \frac{2}{6} \qquad \frac{6}{6}$$

A. $\frac{1}{6} > \frac{4}{6}$ **B.** $\frac{6}{6} < \frac{1}{6}$ **C.** $\frac{3}{6} < \frac{6}{6}$ **D.** $\frac{2}{6} > \frac{4}{6}$

3.NF.A.2.B

20. What fraction can be used to name the point on this number line?

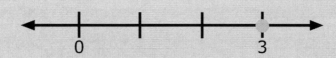

_____

3.NF.A.3.B

prepaze

MEASUREMENT & DATA

www.prepaze.com

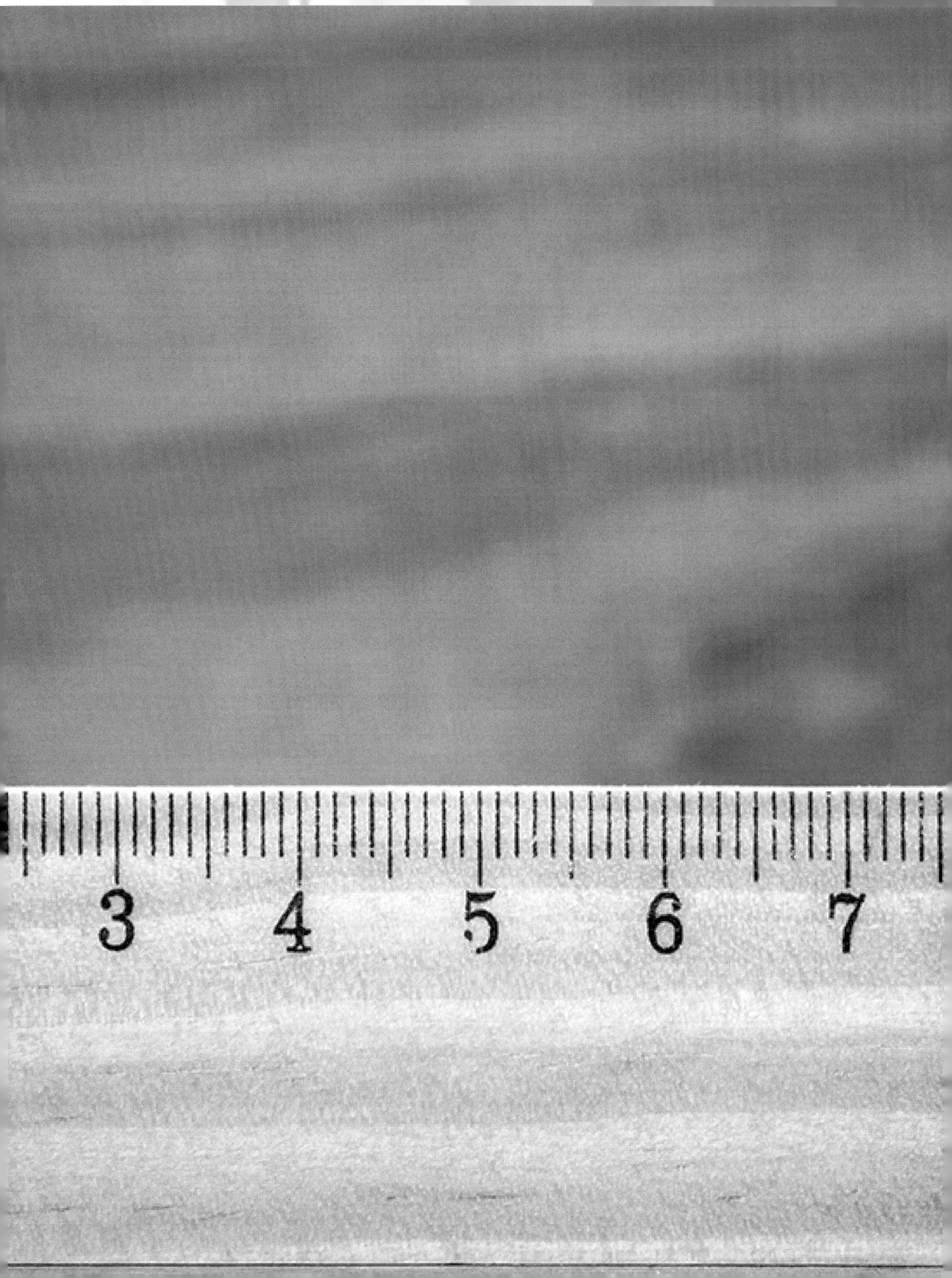
3 4 5 6 7

MEASUREMENT & DATA

1. What time does the clock show?

A. Six o'clock **B.** Seven to seven
C. Seven thirty **D.** Seven after seven

3.MD.A.1

2. In the following recipe for apple crumble, which of these ingredients is needed in the largest amount?

- ½ cup butter

- ¾ cup sugar

- 1 cup flour

- 5 – 6 peeled, sliced apples

- 2 Teaspoons cinnamon

A. Cinnamon **B.** Butter
C. Flour **D.** Sugar

3.MD.A.2

3. What time does the clock show?

A. 3:30 **B.** 3:37
C. 3:15 **D.** 6:19

3.MD.A.1

prepaze

MEASUREMENT & DATA

4. Lindsay kept a log of how many pages she read in the past 3 days. How many pages did she read on Thursday?

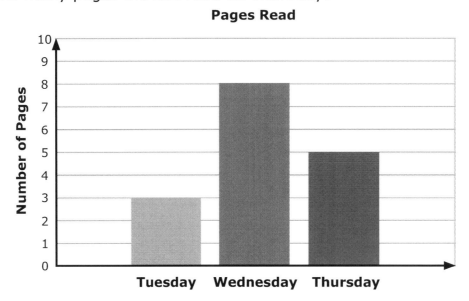

Pages Read

A. 4 pages   **B.** 1 page   **C.** 5 pages   **D.** 0 page

(3.MD.B.3)

5. In the following recipe for turkey dressing, which of these ingredients is needed in the largest amount?

- 3 cups of bread crumbs
- 6 cups of cornbread crumbs
- 3 cups of chicken broth
- ½ cup of diced onions
- ¼ cup of diced celery
- 2 Teaspoons sage

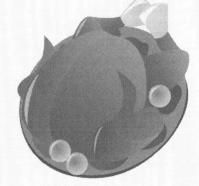

A. Bread crumbs   **B.** Cornbread crumbs
C. Chicken broth   **D.** Sage

(3.MD.A.2)

MEASUREMENT & DATA

6. What time does the clock show?

A. Thirty-eight past Eleven   **B.** Eleven o'clock
C. Ten thirty   **D.** Thirty-eight to Eleven

3.MD.A.1

7. Some students compared how many trophies they had. How many trophies does Clint have?

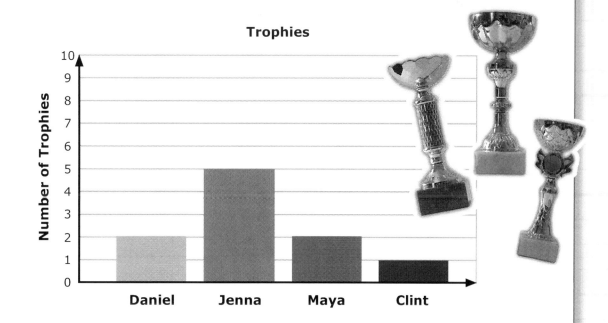

A. 5 trophies   **B.** 6 trophies
C. 2 trophies   **D.** 1 trophy

3.MD.B.3

prepaze

108   NAME: ....   DATE: ....

MEASUREMENT & DATA

ESTIMATING MEASUREMENT & GRAPHS

8. Mrs. Rosner wanted to see how many miles she drove each day. How many miles did she drive on Friday?

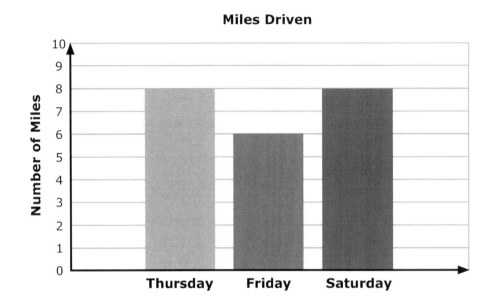

Miles Driven

A. 8 miles   **B.** 6 miles   **C.** 5 miles   **D.** 4 miles

3.MD.B.3

9. Which digital clock shows the same time as this analog clock?

A.   **B.**   **C.**   **D.**

3.MD.A.1

MEASUREMENT & DATA

10. In the following recipe for Chili, which of these ingredients is needed in the smallest amount?

- 1 lb ground beef
- ¼ cup onions
- 2 ½ cups cooked pintos
- 1 cup water
- 2 cups tomato juice
- ¼ teaspoon garlic powder
- 1 teaspoon salt
- 3 tablespoons chili powder

A. Onions   **B.** Chili powder
C. Tomato Juice   **D.** Garlic Powder

3.MD.A.2

11. Lindsay set her alarm to go off so she could get to school on time. Is it AM or PM?

A. A.M.   **B.** P.M.

3.MD.A.1

ESTIMATING MEASUREMENT & GRAPHS

12. Scott wanted to know which state at the best gas prices during the holiday season. Which state had the cheapest gas prices?

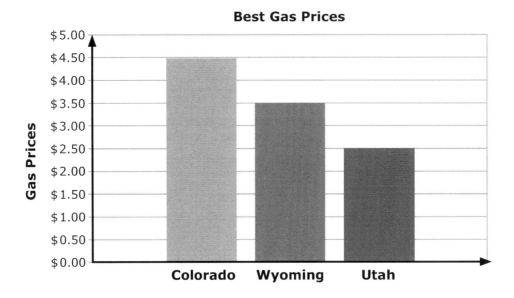

Best Gas Prices

A. Colorado   **B.** Wyoming

C. Utah   **D.** Alaska

3.MD.B.3

13. True or False: Seven grams is a good estimate for the weight of a toaster.

A. True

B. False

3.MD.A.2

MEASUREMENT & DATA

14. Adam kept track of how many kilometers he ran during the past 5 days. Use the data in the table to create a bar graph below.

Kilometers Run	
Day	**Kilometers**
Sunday	5
Monday	1
Tuesday	3
Wednesday	2
Thursday	2

Kilometers Run

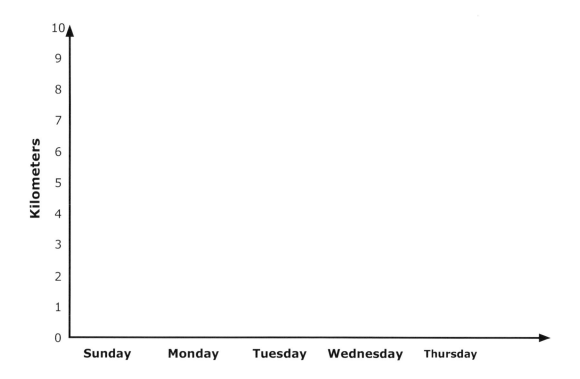

3.MD.B.3

MEASUREMENT & DATA

15. Jared recorded how many pizzas he had made over the past 3 days. Use the data in the chart below to create a bar graph.

Pizzas Made	
Day	**Pizzas**
Sunday	1
Monday	4
Tuesday	9

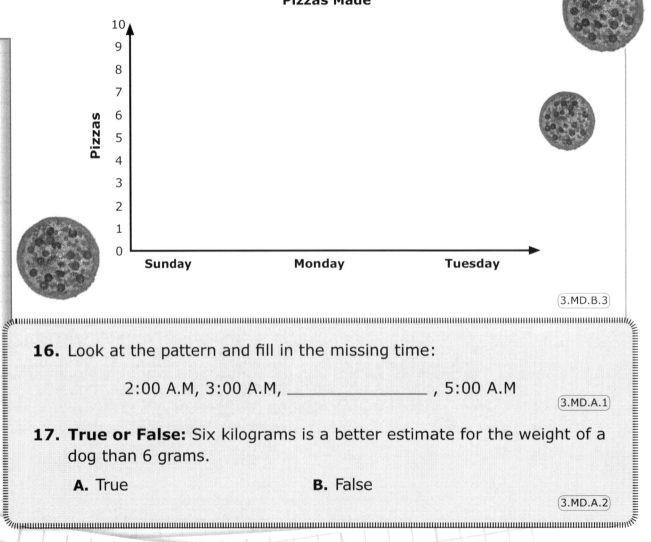

Pizzas Made

3.MD.B.3

16. Look at the pattern and fill in the missing time:

2:00 A.M, 3:00 A.M, _____ , 5:00 A.M

3.MD.A.1

17. True or False: Six kilograms is a better estimate for the weight of a dog than 6 grams.

A. True   **B.** False

3.MD.A.2

MEASUREMENT & DATA

18. Use the data in the tally chart to complete the missing row in the pictograph below. Color in the correct number of books.

Library Books Checked Out	
Month	**Books**
December	卌 卌
January	卌 卌 卌 卌
February	卌 卌
March	卌 卌 卌 卌
April	卌 卌

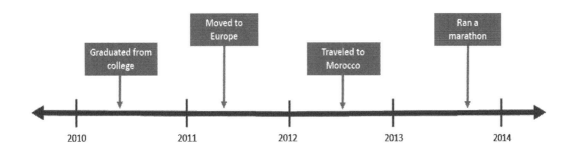

= 10 books

3.MD.B.3

19. Which event on this timeline happened after 2013?

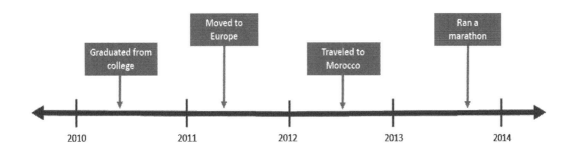

3.MD.A.1

UNIT 2:   MEASURING LENGTH

prepaze

MEASUREMENT & DATA

1. What is the length of this line segment to the nearest inch?

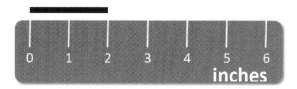

A. 2 inches   **B.** 1 inch   **C.** 4 inches   **D.** 6 inches

3.MD.B.4

2. What is the length of this line segment to the nearest inch?

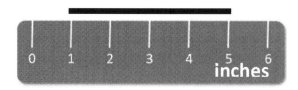

A. 2 inches   **B.** 5 inches   **C.** 3 inches   **D.** 4 inches

3.MD.B.4

3. What is the length of this line segment to the nearest inch?

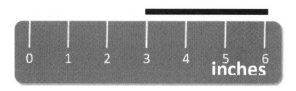

A. 5 inches   **B.** 3 inches   **C.** 4 inches   **D.** 6 inches

3.MD.B.4

MEASUREMENT & DATA

4. What is the length of this line segment to the nearest inch?

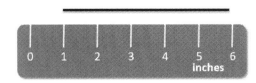

   A. 6 inches   **B.** 3 inches   **C.** 4 inches   **D.** 5 inches

3.MD.B.4

5. What is the length of the sword to the nearest inch?

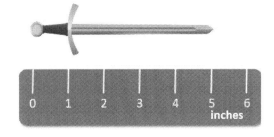

   A. 5 inches   **B.** 4 inches   **C.** 6 inches   **D.** 3 inches

3.MD.B.4

6. What is the length of the tulip to the nearest half inch?

   A. 3 inches   **B.** $2\frac{1}{2}$ inches   **C.** $1\frac{1}{2}$ inches   **D.** 2 inches

3.MD.B.4

prepaze

MEASUREMENT & DATA

MEASURING LENGTH

7. What is the length of the crown to the nearest inch?

A. 6 inches   **B.** 4 inches   **C.** 1 inch   **D.** 2 inches

3.MD.B.4

8. What is the length of the dog to the nearest inch?

A. 6 inches   **B.** 5 inches   **C.** 4 inches   **D.** 3 inches

3.MD.B.4

9. What is the length of this drawing of an orca whale to the nearest inch?

A. 4 inches   **B.** 3 inches   **C.** 6 inches   **D.** 2 inches

3.MD.B.4

SUREMENT & DATA

MEASURING LENGTH

car has a length of 5 inches.

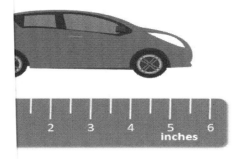

B. False

3.MD.B.4

---

11. True or False: The candy cane has a length of $2\frac{1}{2}$ inches.

A. True   **B.** False

3.MD.B.4

---

12. True or False: The toy shoe has a length of $3\frac{1}{2}$ inches.

A. True   **B.** False

3.MD.B.4

NAME: _____ DATE: _____

MEASUREMENT & DATA

13. True or False: The lizard has a length of 3 inches.

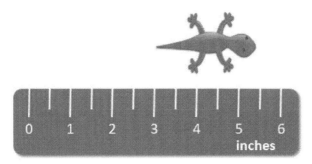

A. True   **B.** False

(3.MD.B.4)

14. True or False: The couch is $2\frac{1}{2}$ yards long.

A. True   **B.** False

(3.MD.B.4)

15. What is the length of the crayon to the nearest $\frac{1}{4}$ of an inch?

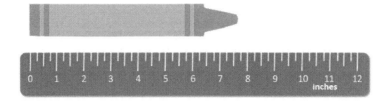

_____ inches

(3.MD.B.4)

MEASUREMENT & DATA

16. What is the length of the candle to the nearest $\frac{1}{4}$ of an inch?

_____ inches

(3.MD.B.4)

17. What is the length of the lollipop to the nearest $\frac{1}{4}$ of an inch?

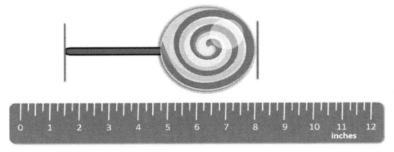

_____ inches

(3.MD.B.4)

18. What is the length of the crab to the nearest $\frac{1}{4}$ of an inch?

_____ inches

(3.MD.B.4)

prepaze

MEASUREMENT & DATA

MEASURING LENGTH

19. What is the length of the toaster to the nearest $\frac{1}{4}$ of an inch?

_____ inches

3.MD.B.4

20. What is the length of the gift box to the nearest $\frac{1}{4}$ of an inch?

_____ inches

3.MD.B.4

UNIT 3: AREA AND PERIMETER

MEASUREMENT & DATA

1. What is the area of this rectangle?

3 units

2 units

   A. 1 square unit   **B.** 6 square units

   C. 10 square units   **D.** 5 square units

3.MD.C.7

2. The following shape is made of unit squares. Determine the area of the shape.

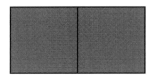

   A. 3 square units   **B.** 2 square units

   C. 5 square units   **D.** $\frac{1}{2}$ square unit

3.MD.C.6

3. The following shape is made of unit squares. Determine the area of the shape.

   A. 1 square unit   **B.** 2 square units

   C. 5 square units   **D.** 3 square units

3.MD.C.5

prepaze

MEASUREMENT & DATA

4. What is the perimeter of the rectangle?

4 inches

5 inches

A. 25 inches   **B.** 20 inches

C. 18 inches   **D.** 9 inches

3.MD.D.8

5. The following shape is made of unit squares. Determine the area of the shape.

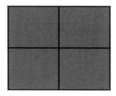

A. 4 square units   **B.** 2 square units

C. 6 square units   **D.** 1 square unit

3.MD.C.6

6. What is the perimeter of this figure?

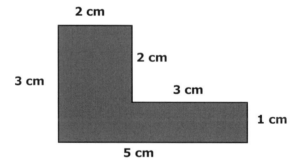

2 cm

2 cm

3 cm

3 cm

1 cm

5 cm

A. 10 cm   **B.** 8 cm

C. 16 cm   **D.** 15 cm

3.MD.D.8

MEASUREMENT & DATA

7. The following shape is made of unit squares. Determine the area of the shape.

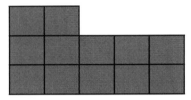

   A. 10 square units   **B.** 8 square units

   C. 12 square units   **D.** 6 square units

3.MD.C.5

8. What is the area of the rectangle?

3 units

5 units

   A. 50 square units   **B.** 20 square units

   C. 45 square units   **D.** 15 square units

3.MD.C.7

9. The following shape is made of unit squares. Determine the area of the shape.

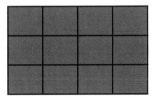

   A. 11 square units   **B.** 15 square units

   C. 12 square units   **D.** 9 square units

3.MD.C.6

prepaze

MEASUREMENT & DATA

10. What is the perimeter of the shape?

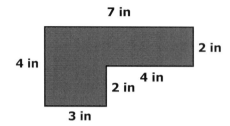

A. 20 in   **B.** 22 in

C. 18 in   **D.** 28 in

3.MD.D.8

11. The following shape is made of unit squares. Determine the area of the shape.

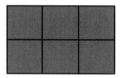

A. 3 square units   **B.** 8 square units

C. 2 square units   **D.** 6 square units

3.MD.C.5

12. The following figure is made of unit squares. Determine the area of the shape.

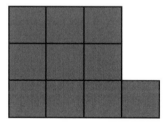

A. 10 square units   **B.** 15 square units

C. 14 square units   **D.** 4 square units

3.MD.C.6

MEASUREMENT & DATA

13. Each square in the following figure has an area of 1 square meter. **True or False:** The total area of the figure can be calculated with this expression: $(3 \times 6) + 3$.

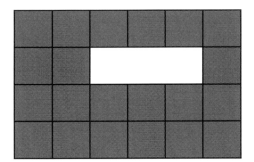

A. True   **B.** False

3.MD.C.7

14. True or False: The following shape has an area of 9 square units. The shape is made of unit squares.

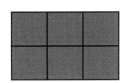

A. True   **B.** False

3.MD.C.6

15. True or False: Each square in the figure has an area of 1 square centimeter. The total area of the blue figure can be determined with this expression:

$$(4 \times 7)$$

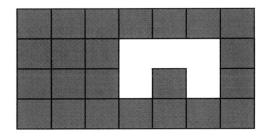

A. True   **B.** False

3.MD.C.7

prepaze

NAME: .... DATE: ....

MEASUREMENT & DATA

16. Which figure has a greater perimeter?

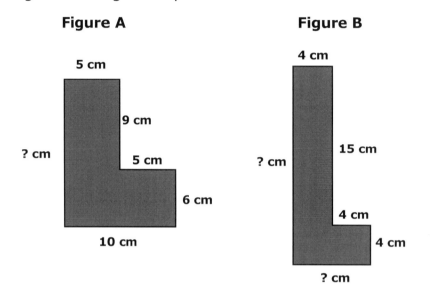

Figure A	Figure B

3.MD.D.8

17. Each square in this drawing represents 1 square unit. What is the area of the drawing?

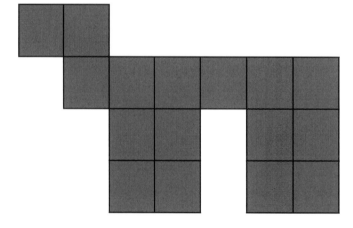

_____ square units

3.MD.C.5

prepaze

www.prepaze.com

MEASUREMENT & DATA

18.

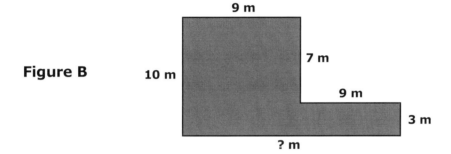

Figure A

6 m

8 m   8 m

10 m

Figure B

9 m

10 m

7 m

9 m

3 m

? m

A. What is the missing length on Figure B? _____

B. Which figure has the greatest perimeter? _____

3.MD.D.8

19. Each square in the following figure has an area of 1 square centimeter.

True or False: The area of the figure can be determined using this expression:

$$(8 \times 3) - (8 - 3)$$

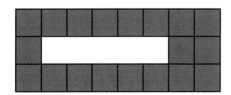

A. True   **B.** False

3.MD.C.7

prepaze

MEASUREMENT & DATA

AREA AND PERIMETER

20. Each square in this drawing represents 1 square unit. What is the area of the drawing?

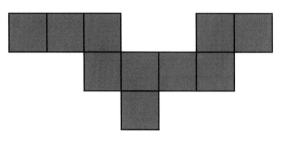

_____ square units

3.MD.C.5

MEASUREMENT & DATA

1. Susan and Lindsay wanted to know how many hours they had worked over the past few days. Which day did they work the least?

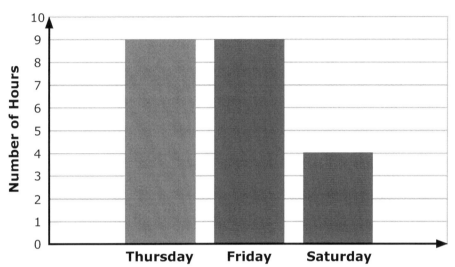

Hours Worked

A. Thursday   **B.** Friday   **C.** Saturday   **D.** Sunday

3.MD.B.3

2. Which is a better unit to use to describe the volume of a bottle of cough syrup?

A. liter   **B.** milliliter
C. kilogram   **D.** gram

3.MD.A.2

3. What is the length of the line segment to the nearest inch?

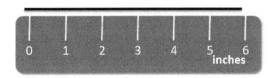

A. 4 inches   **B.** 3 inches   **C.** 6 inches   **D.** 5 inches

3.MD.B.4

prepaze

MEASUREMENT & DATA

4. Each square in this figure has an area of 1 square unit. What is the area of the shaded figure?

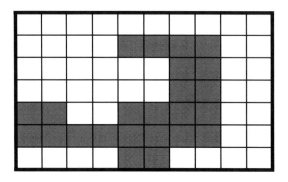

A. 70 square units   **B.** 22 square units
C. 30 square units   **D.** 24 square units

3.MD.C.5.A

5. How many miles were driven on all 3 days combined?

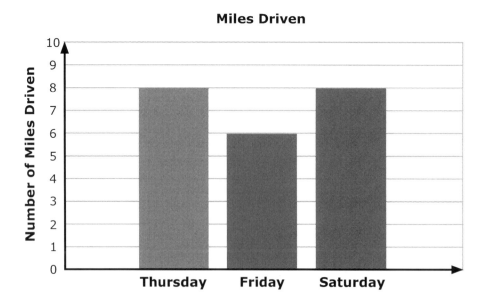

A. 22 miles   **B.** 20 miles   **C.** 16 miles   **D.** 14 miles

3.MD.B.3

MEASUREMENT & DATA

6. What is the area of the rectangle?

4 units

3 units

A. 15 square units

B. 25 square units

C. 12 square units

D. 24 square units

3.MD.C.7

7. Each square in this image is 1 square centimeter. What is the area of the shaded figure in square centimeters?

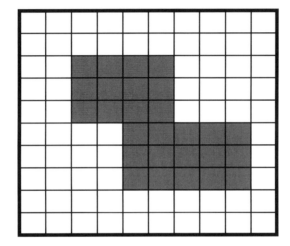

A. 100 square centimeters

C. 15 square centimeters

B. 12 square centimeters

D. 27 square centimeters

3.MD.C.6

8. What time does the clock show?

A. Twelve o'clock

B. Six thirty

C. Six thirteen

D. Two thirty

3.MD.A.1

prepaze

9. What is the perimeter of the rectangle?

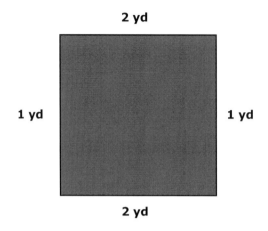

2 yd

1 yd   1 yd

2 yd

A. 2 yds   **B.** 8 yds   **C.** 4 yds   **D.** 6 yds

3.MD.D.8

10. True or False: The fish tank has a length of $5\frac{1}{4}$ yards.

A. True   **B.** False

3.MD.B.4

MEASUREMENT & DATA

11. What is the perimeter of the rectangle?

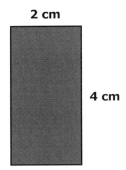

2 cm

4 cm

A. 6 cm   **B.** 12 cm   **C.** 8 cm   **D.** 2 cm

3.MD.D.8

12. Which is a better unit to describe the volume of a plastic grocery bag?

A. liter   **B.** milliliter   **C.** kilogram   **D.** gram

3.MD.A.2

13. What is the perimeter of the figure?

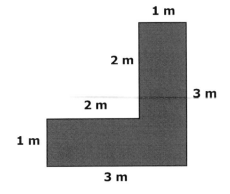

1 m

2 m

3 m

2 m

1 m

3 m

A. 10 m   **B.** 12 m   **C.** 16 m   **D.** 9 m

3.MD.D.8

prepaze

MEASUREMENT & DATA

CHAPTER REVIEW

14. Each square in this image is 1 square centimeter. What is the difference between the area of the entire image and the area of the shaded figure?

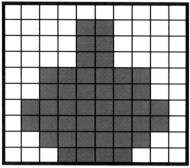

   A. 100 square centimeters   **B.** 44 square centimeters
   C. 56 square centimeters   **D.** 50 square centimeters

3.MD.C.6

15. Maria is the school photographer and keeps a record of how many pictures she takes. Which day did she take the fewest pictures?

Pictures Maria Took

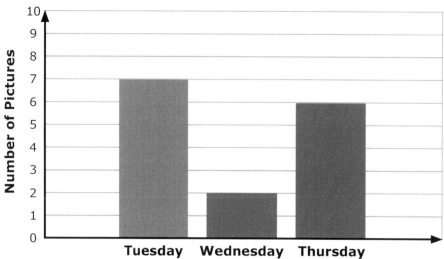

  A. Tuesday   **B.** Monday   **C.** Thursday   **D.** Wednesday

3.MD.B.3

MEASUREMENT & DATA

16. What is the area of the rectangle?

7 units

4 units

A. 32 square units **B.** 12 square units
C. 22 square units **D.** 28 square units

3.MD.C.7

17. This image of an ice cream cone is $4\frac{1}{2}$ inches in length.

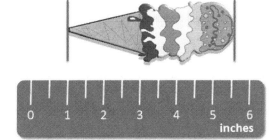

A. True **B.** False

3.MD.B.4

18. Which digital clock shows the same time as the analog clock?

A. **B.** **C.** **D.**

3.MD.A.1

MEASUREMENT & DATA

19. Each square in these rectangles has an area of 1 square meter.

| **A.** | **B.** | **C.** | **D.** |

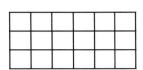 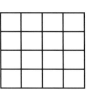 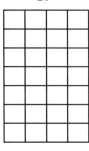 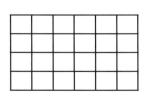

Which rectangle has the greatest area?

A. Rectangle A   **B.** Rectangle B

C. Rectangle C   **D.** Rectangle D

3.MD.C.6

20. Each square in this figure has an area of 1 square unit.

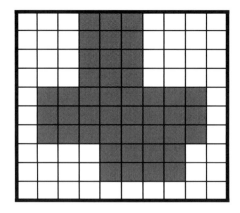

What is the area of the shaded figure?

A. 70 square units   **B.** 44 square units

C. 30 square units   **D.** 24 square units

3.MD.C.5.A

EXTRA PRACTICE

prepaze   www.prepaze.com

MEASUREMENT & DATA

1. What is the perimeter of the shape?

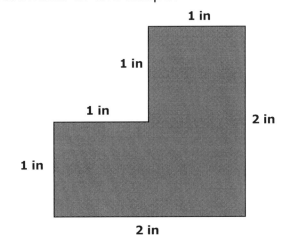

A. 10 in   **B.** 4 in   **C.** 2 in   **D.** 8 in

3.MD.D.8

2. Which is a better unit to describe the volume of a kitchen sink?

A. liter   **B.** milliliter   **C.** kilogram   **D.** gram

3.MD.A.2

3. **True or False:** The perimeter of the following shape is 11 ft.

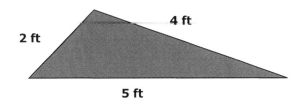

A. True   **B.** False

3.MD.D.8

prepaze

MEASUREMENT & DATA

4. **True or False:** The image of the duck measures 3 inches in length.

A. True   **B.** False

3.MD.B.4

5. **True or False:** The area of the shape below is 14 square units. Each square has an area of 1 square unit.

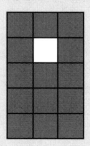

A. True   **B.** False

3.MD.C.7

6. Joshua uses these gray squares to begin measuring the area of this figure.

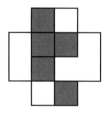

He runs out of squares, but knows each square has an area of 1 square unit. What is the area of the figure?

A. 5 square units   **B.** 7 square units
C. 12 square units   **D.** 8 square units

3.MD.C.5.B

MEASUREMENT & DATA

7. How many pages did Lindsay read on Wednesday and Thursday combined?

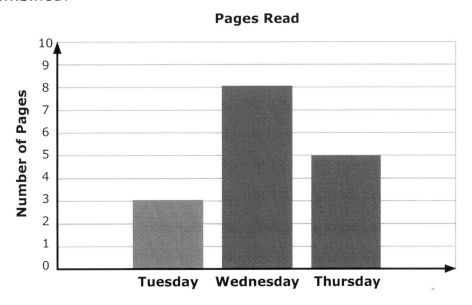

Pages Read

A. 9 pages   **B.** 13 pages   **C.** 5 pages   **D.** 16 pages

3.MD.B.3

8. What is the area of this rectangle?

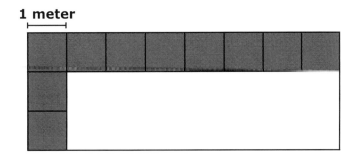

1 meter

A. 11 square meters   **B.** 22 square meters
C. 16 square meters   **D.** 24 square meters

3.MD.C.6

MEASUREMENT & DATA

EXTRA PRACTICE

9. What time does the clock show?

A. 11:02   **B.** 2:55

C. 11:09   **D.** 2:11

3.MD.A.1

10. Each square in this figure has an area of 1 square unit.

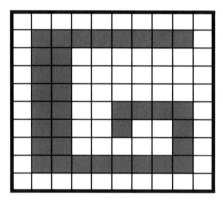

What is the area of the shaded figure?

A. 70 square units   **B.** 16 square units

C. 35 square units   **D.** 24 square units

3.MD.C.5.A

11. The surface of a rectangular table is 6 feet long and 2 feet wide. What is its area?

_____ square feet

3.MD.C.7

prepaze

MEASUREMENT & DATA

12. Five milliliters is a better estimate for the volume of a dose of cough syrup than 5 liters.

A. True   **B.** False

3.MD.A.2

13. What is the area of this figure?

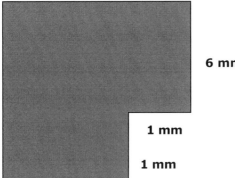

6 mm

6 mm

1 mm

1 mm

5 mm

_____ square mm

3.MD.C.7

14. What is the area of this rectangle?

1 meter

_____ square units

3.MD.C.6

prepaze

MEASUREMENT & DATA

15. Steve uses the gray squares to begin finding the area of this figure. Each square has an area of 1 square unit. What is the area of the figure?

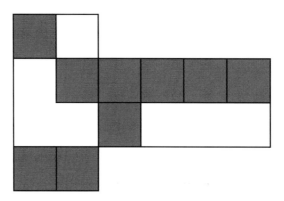

_____ square units

3.MD.C.5.B

16. This is Trent's timeline. Around what time did he return his library books?

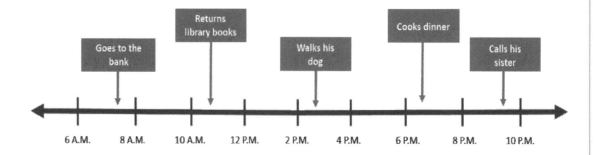

3.MD.A.1

MEASUREMENT & DATA

17. Use the data in the tally chart to complete the missing row in the pictograph below. How many cookies should be added to the picture graph for Alfonso?

Baking Competition	
Name	Batches
Alfonso	𝍷𝍷𝍷
Richard	𝍷𝍷
Saeed	𝍷𝍷𝍷
Raul	𝍷𝍷

Baking Competition	
Alfonso	⬤⬤⬤⬤⬤⬤⬤⬤
Richard	⬤⬤⬤⬤⬤◖
Saeed	⬤⬤⬤⬤⬤⬤
Raul	⬤⬤⬤⬤⬤

⬤ = 2 batches of cookies

◖ = 1 batch of cookies

3.MD.B.3

18. This is Denzel's timeline. Around what time did he watch a movie?

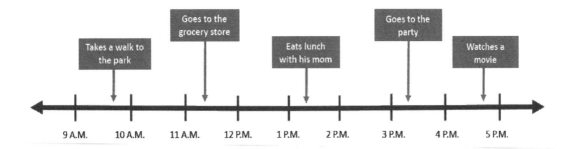

3.MD.A.1

19. Fifty meters is a better estimate for the length of a car key than 50 millimeters.

A. True   **B.** False

3.MD.A.2

prepaze

NAME: ....

DATE: ....

MEASUREMENT & DATA

20. What are the length and width of this rectangle?

_____

3.MD.B.4

GEOMETRY

prepaze

www.prepaze.com

GEOMETRY

1. Which shape is a parallelogram?

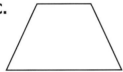

A.

B.

C.

D.

3.G.A.1

2. How many pairs of opposite sides are parallel?

A. No pairs
C. 2 pairs

B. 1 pair
D. 4 pairs

3.G.A.1

3. What shape is this?

A. Hexagon
C. Octagon

B. Pentagon
D. Rhombus

3.G.A.1

prepaze

GEOMETRY

UNDERSTANDING SHAPES

4. How many pairs of opposite sides are parallel?

A. No pairs   **B.** 1 pair   **C.** 2 pairs   **D.** 4 pairs

3.G.A.1

5. Which shape is NOT a parallelogram?

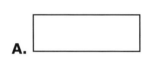 **A.**   **B.**   **C.** 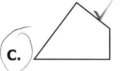   **D.**

3.G.A.1

6. Which shape is a trapezoid?

A.    **B.**    **C.**   **D.**

3.G.A.1

7. How many pairs of opposite sides are parallel?

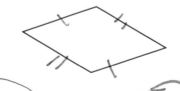

A. No pairs   **B.** 1 pair   **C.** 2 pairs   **D.** 4 pairs

3.G.A.1

prepaze

www.prepaze.com

GEOMETRY

8. Select all the trapezoids.

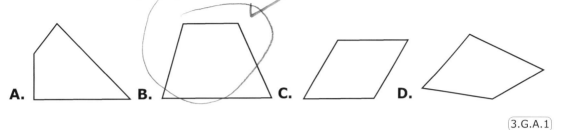

A. B. C. D.

3.G.A.1

9. Select all the rectangles.

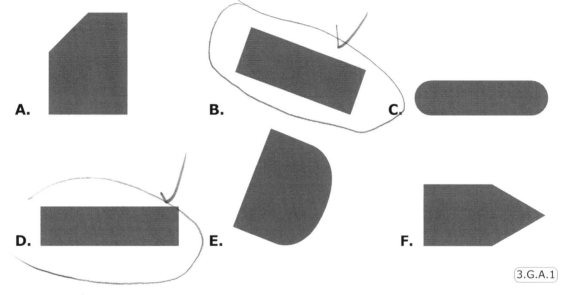

A. B. C.

D. E. F.

3.G.A.1

10. True or False: Only shapes I and III are parallelograms.

I. II. III.

A. True **B.** False

3.G.A.1

prepaze

GEOMETRY

11. True or False: There are no pairs of opposite sides that are parallel in the following shape.

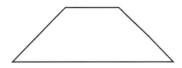

A. True   **B.** False

3.G.A.1

12. What shape is this?

A. Square
B. Kite
C. Parallelogram
D. Rhombus

3.G.A.1

13. What shape is this?

A. Quadrilateral
B. Pentagon
C. Circle
D. Triangle

3.G.A.1

14. How many vertices does this shape have?

_____ vertices

3.G.A.1

15. How many pairs of opposite sides are parallel?

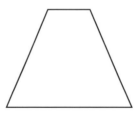

_____ pairs.

3.G.A.1

prepaze

GEOMETRY

16. How many pairs of opposite sides are parallel?

_____ pairs

3.G.A.1

17. How many pairs of opposite sides are parallel?

_____ pairs

3.G.A.1

18. Which attributes of these shapes are the same?

_____

3.G.A.1

19. Draw and label 4 different quadrilaterals.

3.G.A.1

20. Draw and label 3 different parallelograms.

3.G.A.1

UNDERSTANDING SHAPES

UNIT 2:   PARTITION SHAPES

prepaze

NAME: .... DATE: ....

GEOMETRY

PARTITION SHAPES

1. Which shape shows the fraction $\frac{1}{8}$?

 A.   **B.** **C.**   **D.**

3.G.A.2

2. Which shape shows the fraction $\frac{1}{6}$?

 A. **B.**   **C.**   **D.**

3.G.A.2

3. What fraction of the shape is shaded?

A. $\frac{1}{6}$ B. $\frac{3}{6}$

C. $\frac{1}{8}$ D. $\frac{1}{5}$

3.G.A.2

4. Which shape shows the fraction $\frac{1}{3}$?

 A.   **B.**   **C.**   **D.**

3.G.A.2

5. Which shape shows the fraction $\frac{1}{4}$?

 A.   **B.**   **C.**   **D.**

3.G.A.2

prepaze

www.prepaze.com

GEOMETRY

6. What fraction of the shape is shaded?

A. $\frac{1}{4}$ B. $\frac{1}{3}$

C. $\frac{1}{1}$ D. $\frac{1}{2}$

3.G.A.2

7. What fraction of the shape is shaded?

A. 1   B. $\frac{2}{3}$

C. $\frac{3}{3}$ D. $\frac{1}{3}$

3.G.A.2

8. What fraction of the shape is shaded?

A. $\frac{1}{2}$ B. $\frac{1}{3}$

C. $\frac{1}{4}$ D. $\frac{1}{5}$

3.G.A.2

9. Which shape shows the fraction $\frac{1}{2}$?

A.   B.   C.   D.

3.G.A.2

10. What fraction of the shape is shaded?

A. $\frac{3}{4}$ B. $\frac{2}{4}$

C. $\frac{1}{4}$ D. $\frac{1}{2}$

3.G.A.2

GEOMETRY

PARTITION SHAPES

11. What fraction of the shape is shaded?

    A. $\frac{1}{4}$ **B.** $\frac{7}{8}$

    C. $\frac{1}{2}$ **D.** $\frac{1}{8}$

3.G.A.2

12. What fraction of the shape is shaded?

    A. $\frac{1}{2}$ **B.** $\frac{1}{4}$

    C. $\frac{1}{3}$ **D.** $\frac{1}{5}$

3.G.A.2

13. Which shape shows the fraction $\frac{1}{4}$?

A.   **B.**   **C.**   **D.**

3.G.A.2

14. True or False: The fraction in Model B is greater than the fraction shown in Model A.

    Model A   **Model B**

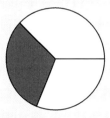   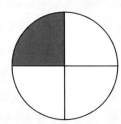

    A. True   **B.** False

3.G.A.2

GEOMETRY

15. What unit fraction is represented by the shaded area?

_____

(3.G.A.2)

16. What unit fraction is represented by the shaded area?

_____

(3.G.A.2)

17. What fraction of the shape is shaded?

_____

(3.G.A.2)

18. What fraction of the shape is shaded?

_____

(3.G.A.2)

prepaze

GEOMETRY

PARTITION SHAPES

19. Explain why the shaded part of this model represents $\frac{1}{6}$?

_____

_____

_____

_____

3.G.A.2

20. Explain why the shaded part of this model represents $\frac{1}{8}$?

_____

_____

_____

_____

3.G.A.2

CHAPTER REVIEW

GEOMETRY

1. Which quadrilateral has 4 right angles?

   A. Kite   **B.** Rectangle   **C.** Trapezoid   **D.** Rhombus

   (3.G.A.1)

2. Which unit fraction represents each part of the whole shown below?

   A. $\frac{1}{3}$ **B.** $\frac{1}{6}$ **C.** $\frac{1}{4}$ **D.** $\frac{1}{8}$

   (3.G.A.2)

3. Which statement correctly describes a parallelogram?

   A. A parallelogram is a four-sided shape with only one pair of opposite sides.

   B. A parallelogram is a shape whose diagonals are parallel.

   C. A parallelogram is a four-sided shape whose opposite sides are parallel.

   D. A parallelogram is a shape whose angles are parallel.

   (3.G.A.1)

4. Which unit fraction represents each part of the whole shown below?

   A. $\frac{1}{3}$ **B.** $\frac{1}{6}$ **C.** $\frac{1}{4}$ **D.** $\frac{1}{8}$

   (3.G.A.2)

5. Which quadrilateral has no right angles?

   A. Square   **B.** Rhombus   **C.** Rectangle   **D.** Trapezoid

   (3.G.A.1)

prepaze

GEOMETRY

6. How many $\frac{1}{4}$ parts of this model are shaded?

    A. 3   **B.** 4   **C.** 2   **D.** 1

3.G.A.2

7. Mr. Jones cuts this pie into pieces of equal size.

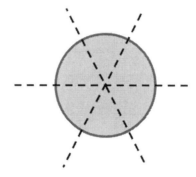

What fraction of the whole pie does each piece represent?

    A. $\frac{1}{3}$ **B.** $\frac{1}{6}$ **C.** $\frac{1}{4}$ **D.** $\frac{1}{8}$

3.G.A.2

8. Elizabeth cuts this apple into 2 pieces of equal size.

What fraction names the size of one part?

    A. $\frac{1}{3}$ **B.** $\frac{1}{6}$ **C.** $\frac{1}{2}$ **D.** $\frac{1}{1}$

3.G.A.2

GEOMETRY

9. Which name does NOT describe this shape?

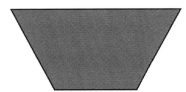

A. Kite

B. Trapezoid

C. Polygon

D. Quadrilateral

3.G.A.1

10. Which quadrilateral has only 2 sides that are the same length?

A. Isosceles trapezoid

B. Parallelogram

C. Square

D. Rhombus

3.G.A.1

11. What is the unit fraction of the model shown below?

A. $\frac{1}{3}$

B. $\frac{1}{6}$

C. $\frac{1}{4}$

D. $\frac{1}{8}$

3.G.A.2

12. Which name does NOT describe this shape?

A. Polygon

B. Quadrilateral

C. Heptagon

D. Parallelogram

3.G.A.1

prepaze

GEOMETRY

13. Thomas made this game board. Each square has the same area.

Start			

Which fraction is represented by the shaded part of the game board?

A. $\frac{10}{1}$ **B.** $\frac{1}{9}$ **C.** $\frac{9}{1}$ **D.** $\frac{1}{10}$

(3.G.A.2)

14. Which shape is a rectangle?

A. **B.** **C.** **D. None**

(3.G.A.1)

15. What fraction describes the shaded part of this model?

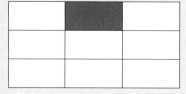

A. $\frac{1}{8}$ **B.** $\frac{1}{9}$ **C.** $\frac{1}{3}$ **D.** $\frac{1}{2}$

(3.G.A.2)

16. Which shape has more sides?

A. **B.** **C.** **D.**

(3.G.A.1)

GEOMETRY

17. What unit fraction represents each part of the whole for this model?

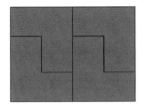

A. $\frac{1}{8}$ B. $\frac{1}{4}$

C. $\frac{1}{3}$ D. $\frac{1}{2}$

3.G.A.2

18. Select all the trapezoids.

 A.    **B.**   **C.**    **D.**

3.G.A.1

19. True or False: There are no pairs of opposite sides that are parallel in the following figure.

A. True   **B.** False

3.G.A.1

20. Which model shows a unit fraction greater than $\frac{1}{3}$?

A.   **B.**   **C.**   **D.**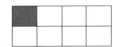

3.G.A.2

EXTRA PRACTICE

prepaze

GEOMETRY

EXTRA PRACTICE

1. Which model shows a unit fraction less than $\frac{1}{6}$?

 A.   **B.**    **C.**    **D.**

3.G.A.2

2. Which model shows the unit fraction $\frac{1}{4}$?

 **A.**   **B.**   **C.**   **D.**

3.G.A.2

3. **True or False:** There are 2 pairs of opposite sides that are parallel in the following figure.

A. True   **B.** False

3.G.A.1

4. **True or False:** Figures I and II are trapezoids.

 I.   **II.**    **III.**

A. True   **B.** False

3.G.A.1

GEOMETRY

5. How many pairs of parallel sides does this shape have?

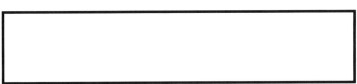

3.G.A.1

6. Carrie draws a model where the unit fraction is $\frac{1}{6}$. How many parts does Carrie's model have?

3.G.A.2

7. How many more right angles does Shape A have than Shape B?

Shape A

Shape B

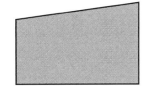

3.G.A.1

8. Michael says these fractions are unit fractions because they all have the same numbers. Do you agree with Michael? Explain your reasoning.

$$\frac{1}{3} \qquad \frac{3}{4} \qquad \frac{1}{4}$$

3.G.A.2

prepaze

GEOMETRY

EXTRA PRACTICE

9. Jane says every quadrilateral is a parallelogram. Do you agree with Jane? Explain your reasoning.

_____

_____

_____

3.G.A.1

10. Model the unit fraction $\frac{1}{8}$ using the rectangle below.

3.G.A.2

11. What fraction is represented by the model below?

_____

3.G.A.2

12. Draw two polygons with more than 4 sides.

3.G.A.1

GEOMETRY

13. Fill in the blank.

A quadrilateral with only one pair of parallel sides is called a

_____.

(3.G.A.1)

14. What unit fraction is represented by the model below?

_____

(3.G.A.2)

15. How would you describe the relationship between the angles in a square and the angles in a rectangle?

_____

_____

_____

(3.G.A.1)

16. Color $\frac{1}{3}$ of each shape.

(3.G.A.2)

prepaze

GEOMETRY

17. Andrea draws this diagram to show how she would organize four-sided shapes.

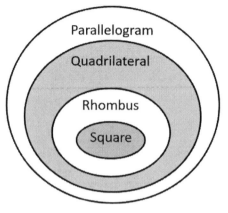

Do you agree with Andrea's diagram? Explain your reasoning.

_____

_____

_____

3.G.A.1

18. Jalinda says this model represents $\frac{1}{2}$ because the whole is divided into 2 pieces. Do you agree with Jalinda? Explain your reasoning.

_____

_____

_____

3.G.A.2

GEOMETRY

19. Brian creates this Venn diagram to compare quadrilaterals.

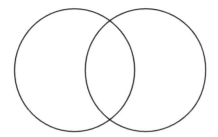

Draw a picture of a rectangle and a trapezoid in the right part of this diagram.

3.G.A.1

20. Isaiah says the only fraction which can be modeled with a hexagon are sixths because a hexagon has six sides.

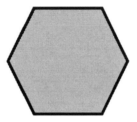

Do you agree with Isaiah? Explain your reasoning.

_____

_____

_____

3.G.A.2

prepaze

COMPREHENSIVE ASSESSMENTS

ASSESSMENT ①

COMPREHENSIVE ASSESSMENTS

1. Use the array below to help you find the unknown number in $7 = n \div 3$.

A. 21 **B.** 14

C. 24 **D.** 18

3.OA.A.4

2. Using the commutative property, find the correct multiplication facts to match the array below.

A. 3×4 and 4×3

B. 4×5 and 5×4

C. 2×6 and 6×2

D. 3×2 and 2×3

3.OA.B.5

3. Which multiplication equation can be used to count the total number of apples in this picture?

A. $3 \times 4 =$

B. $4 \times 4 =$

C. $3 \times 3 =$

D. $4 + 4 =$

3.OA.A.1

prepaze

COMPREHENSIVE ASSESSMENTS

ASSESSMENT 1

4. Each square has a value of 7. Find the value of the 5 squares.

A. 28   **B.** 35
C. 30   **D.** 42

(3.OA.C.7)

5. A shopping bag with 10 apples weighs 190 ounces. If the empty shopping bag weighs 10 ounces, how much does each apple weigh?

A. 18 ounces

B. 90 ounces

C. 80 ounces

D. 100 ounces

(3.NBT.A.3)

6. What time does the clock show?

A. 3:20

B. 4:16

C. 3:15

D. 4:03

(3.MD.A.1)

7. Ben walks around a circular yard. It takes him 15 minutes to completely walk 1 time around. How many minutes will it take to complete 5 circles around the yard?

A. 20 minutes   **B.** 75 minutes
C. 15 minutes   **D.** 3 minutes

(3.OA.A.3)

prepaze

COMPREHENSIVE ASSESSMENTS

8. Usain bought 10 bananas at the store. He gives $\frac{1}{5}$ of the bananas to his grandmother. Which model shows the fraction of bananas Usain gave to his grandmother?

A.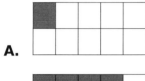

B.

C.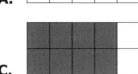

D.

3.NF.A.3.A

ASSESSMENT 1

9. The following shape is made of unit squares. Determine the area of the shape.

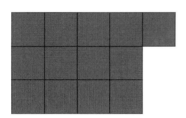

A. 11 square units
B. 15 square units
C. 13 square units
D. 12 square units

3.MD.C.5.A

10. Use the model to help you solve the equation $9 \div 3 =$

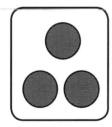 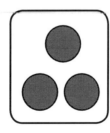 

A. 9   **B.** 6   **C.** 12   **D.** 3

3.OA.B.6

COMPREHENSIVE ASSESSMENTS

ASSESSMENT 1

11. 5 times an even number will always result in a product that is:

A. Odd **B.** Both even and odd
C. Even **D.** Prime

3.OA.D.9

12. Which fraction will complete this inequality?

$$\frac{3}{4} > \underline{\hspace{2cm}}$$

A. $\frac{3}{2}$ **B.** $\frac{3}{5}$ **C.** $\frac{3}{1}$ **D.** $\frac{3}{3}$

3.NF.A.3.D

13. At the fair, Casey bought 3 s'mores and 3 cheesecakes. How much money did he spend on the s'mores and cheesecakes? The following chart shows the unit price for candies.

CANDY	PRICE
Chocolate Bar	$2
S'more	$4
Cheesecake	$7
Tray of cookies	$9

A. $22 **B.** $30
C. $18 **D.** $33

3.OA.A.1

14. Danesha uses unit squares to cover this shape. Each square has an area of one square unit. What is the area of this shape?

A. 10 square units
B. 8 square units
C. 6 square units
D. 4 square units

3.MD.C.5.B

prepaze www.prepaze.com

COMPREHENSIVE ASSESSMENTS

15. Carla made 12 chocolate cupcakes and 12 vanilla cupcakes. She split up all the cupcakes and gave 4 friends the same number of cupcakes. How many cupcakes did each friend receive?

A. 6 cupcakes

B. 8 cupcakes

C. 7 cupcakes

D. 5 cupcakes

3.OA.D.8

16. Jimmy has 56 dog biscuits. He wants to give his 2 dogs an equal number of biscuits each day of the week. How many biscuits will each dog receive per day?

A. 7

B. 4

C. 10

D. 8

3.OA.A.2

ASSESSMENT ①

17. Using the commutative property, find the correct multiplication facts to match the array below.

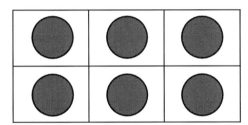

A. 3×4 and 4×3

B. 4×5 and 5×4

C. 2×6 and 6×2

D. 3×2 and 2×3

3.OA.B.5

18. What fraction names the shaded part of this model?

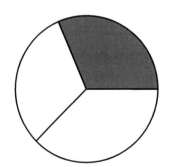

A. $\frac{2}{1}$ **B.** $\frac{2}{3}$

C. $\frac{1}{3}$ **D.** $\frac{1}{2}$

3.NF.A.1

prepaze

COMPREHENSIVE ASSESSMENTS

ASSESSMENT 1

19. What is the area of the rectangle?

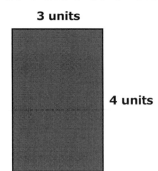

3 units

4 units

A. 12 square units

B. 20 square units

C. 7 square units

D. 24 square units

3.MD.C.7

20. Which multiplication equation matches this model?

A. $4+4$ **B.** 2×3

C. 4×4 **D.** 4×2

3.OA.A.1

21. What is the perimeter of the rectangle?

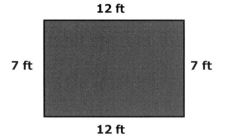

12 ft

7 ft   7 ft

12 ft

A. 14 ft   **B.** 26 ft

C. 38 ft   **D.** 84 ft

3.MD.D.8

22. Shelly is making beaded necklaces. If she uses 10 beads on 6 necklaces, how many beads does she need?

A. $10 \times 6 = 60$ beads   **B.** $6 + 10 = 16$ beads

C. $10 - 6 = 4$ beads   **D.** $10 \div 6 = 2$ beads

3.OA.A.4

COMPREHENSIVE ASSESSMENTS

23. What shape is this?

A. Hexagon   **B.** Pentagon
C. Octagon   **D.** Rhombus

(3.G.A.1)

24. Renee needs paper cups for a party. She buys 4 packs of 40 cups. How many paper cups did Renee buy?

A. 150 paper cups   **B.** 180 paper cups
C. 190 paper cups   **D.** 160 paper cups

(3.NBT.A.3)

25. Where is Point F located?

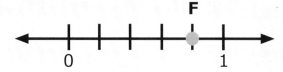

A. $\dfrac{5}{1}$ **B.** 1   **C.** $\dfrac{4}{1}$ **D.** $\dfrac{4}{5}$

(3.NF.A.2.B)

26. In the following recipe for Hot Cocoa, does the recipe call for more sugar or more cocoa?

- ½ cup sugar
- ⅓ cup cocoa
- 4 cups milk
- 1 teaspoon vanilla extract

A. Sugar   **B.** Cocoa

(3.MD.A.2)

prepaze

COMPREHENSIVE ASSESSMENTS

27. Harold has 25 fewer apples than Brea. Brea rounds the number of apples she has to the nearest ten and has about 40 apples. Which number could represent the number of apples Harold has?

_____

3.NBT.A.1

28. What is the area of the rectangle?

8 units

4 units

A. 32 square units   **B.** 12 square units
C. 36 square units   **D.** 24 square units

3.MD.C.7

29. Which shape shows the fraction $\frac{1}{8}$?

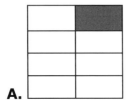 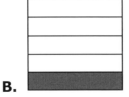  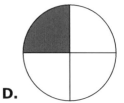

A.   B.   C.   D.

3.G.A.2

COMPREHENSIVE ASSESSMENTS

30. Liam and Sophia are reading the same book.

- ▫ The book has a total of 238 pages.
- ▫ Liam must read 111 pages to finish the book.
- ▫ Sophia must read 182 pages to finish the book.

Explain how you would determine the total number of pages Liam and Sophia have read.

_____

_____

_____

3.NBT.A.2

31. Sally draws this model to show $\frac{2}{8} = \frac{3}{9}$. Do you agree with Sally? Explain your reasoning.

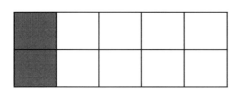   

_____

_____

_____

3.NF.A.3.B

prepaze

COMPREHENSIVE ASSESSMENTS

ASSESSMENT 1

32. Draw a model to show a fraction equivalent to $\frac{2}{6}$.

3.NF.A.3.A

33. Henrietta believes this model represents $\frac{1}{3}$.
Do you agree with Henrietta? Explain your reasoning.

_____

_____

_____

3.G.A.2

34. Model the division statement $12 \div 6$.

3.OA.A.2

35. How many pairs of opposite sides are parallel?

_____ pairs.

3.G.A.1

COMPREHENSIVE ASSESSMENTS

36. Where is $\frac{1}{3}$ on this number line? Place an "X" on the hashmark that represents $\frac{1}{3}$.

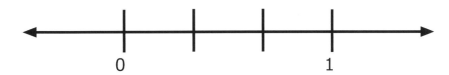

3.NF.A.2.A

37. Use the data in the table to complete the missing row in the picture graph below. Color the dollar signs in.

Weekly Allowances	
Name	**Allowance**
Luigi	$10
Brooke	$40
Clark	$30

Weekly Allowances	
Luigi	$
Brooke	$ $ $ $ $ $ $
Clark	$ $ $

$ = $10

3.MD.B.3

38. Callie's living room is 10 feet wide and 22 feet long. She wants to put a border around the room. The cost of the border is $1.00 per foot. How much will it cost to buy enough of the border to go around the room?

_____

3.MD.D.8

39. Irene did 8 push-ups every day until she reached 48 push-ups. Write a multiplication equation to represent the number of days Irene did push-ups.

_____

3.OA.A.3

prepaze

COMPREHENSIVE ASSESSMENTS

40. What is the area of the square?

2 centimeters

2 centimeters

_____ square centimeters

3.MD.C.7

41. How can 8×8 help you solve 8×7?

_____

_____

_____

3.OA.D.9

42. On the number line below, show how many jumps of 6 are needed to reach 42 from 0.

Write a multiplication equation that represents this problem.

_____

3.OA.C.7

COMPREHENSIVE ASSESSMENTS

43. Explain why this model represents 4 and $\frac{4}{1}$.

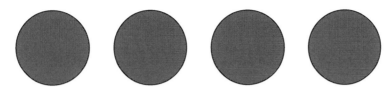

_____

_____

3.NF.A.3.C

44. A building company places concrete blocks around the new school playground. Each block has an area of 1 square foot.

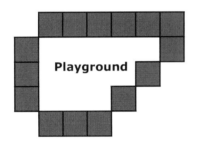

What is the area of the playground?

_____ square feet

3.MD.C.6

45. What is the length of this envelope to the nearest $\frac{4}{1}$ inch?

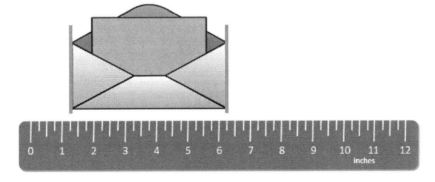

_____

3.MD.B.4

ASSESSMENT 1

prepaze

ASSESSMENT

COMPREHENSIVE ASSESSMENTS

1. Anthony gets 36 new toy cars. If the toy cars come in packs of 4, how many packs of toy cars did Anthony get?

    A. 40 cars   **B.** 32 cars   **C.** 9 cars   **D.** 8 cars

3.OA.A.3

2. Which fraction describes the point on this number line?

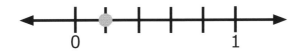

    A. $\frac{4}{1}$ **B.** $\frac{1}{5}$ **C.** $\frac{2}{6}$ **D.** $\frac{2}{4}$

3.NF.A.2.A

3. Lucas makes an array using 3 rows of 5 stickers. How many stickers does Lucas have if he adds 2 more rows to the array?

    A. 15   **B.** 9   **C.** 20   **D.** 25

3.OA.B.5

4. Wendy draws a fraction model. Each part has the same area. One part of the model is shaded, and 7 parts are not shaded. What fraction has Wendy modeled?

    A. $\frac{1}{7}$ **B.** $\frac{1}{8}$ **C.** $\frac{7}{1}$ **D.** $\frac{8}{1}$

3.NF.A.1

prepaze

COMPREHENSIVE ASSESSMENTS

5. Kristen is leaving the school after basketball practice. Is it AM or PM?

A. A.M. **B.** P.M.

3.MD.A.1

6. Karl uses a number line to count by 6 to reach 54. If he starts at zero, how many times did Karl count by 6 to reach 54?

A. 9 **B.** 8 **C.** 7 **D.** 11

3.OA.C.7

7. Complete the equation.

$$\frac{3}{5} = _____$$

A. $\frac{2}{3}$ **B.** $\frac{1}{2}$ **C.** $\frac{3}{9}$ **D.** $\frac{6}{10}$

3.NF.A.3.B

8. What is the multiplication expression that shows $5 + 5 + 5$?

A. 2×5 **B.** 5×5 **C.** 3×5 **D.** $5 \times 5 \times 5$

3.OA.A.1

COMPREHENSIVE ASSESSMENTS

9. Samuel shares 4 cookies with each of his 5 friends at lunch. How many cookies did Samuel have to share? Choose the equation that represents this problem. Let n represent the total number of cookies.

A. $4+5=n$

B. $n-5=4$

C. $4=n\div5$

D. $5=n\times4$

3.OA.A.4

10. Ava has 24 cookies that she places into 8 bags. Which equation can be used to find the unknown factor in this problem?

A. $24=8\times3$

B. $8\times4=24$

C. $8+16=24$

D. $8=24-16$

3.OA.B.6

11. If there are 60 minutes in 1 hour, how many minutes are in 7 hours and 45 minutes?

A. 420 minutes

B. 745 minutes

C. 465 minutes

D. 145 minutes

3.NBT.A.3

12. The following shape is made of unit squares. Determine the area of the shape.

A. 12 square units

B. 15 square units

C. 14 square units

D. 10 square units

3.MD.C.5.A

prepaze

COMPREHENSIVE ASSESSMENTS

ASSESSMENT ②

13. Trinh's cat has 12 kittens. One-fourth of the kittens have white paws. Which model represents the fraction of kittens with white paws?

A.

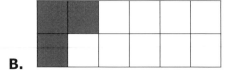

B.

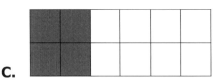

C.

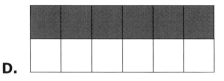

D.

3.NF.A.3.A

14. Mrs. Kilton writes this equation on the board:

$14 \times 3 = (9 \times 3) + ($_____ $\times 3)$. What is the missing number that makes this equation true?

A. 7   **B.** 4   **C.** 6   **D.** 5

3.OA.D.9

15. There are 675 people in Thomas' school. What is this number rounded to the nearest 100?

A. 700   **B.** 600   **C.** 670   **D.** 680

3.NBT.A.1

16. What fraction is equivalent to 5?

A. $\frac{5}{5}$ **B.** $\frac{1}{5}$ **C.** $\frac{5}{1}$ **D.** $\frac{5}{0}$

3.NF.A.3.C

prepaze

COMPREHENSIVE ASSESSMENTS

17. One day at lunch, a restaurant served 178 burgers, 63 grilled cheese sandwiches, and 37 salads. Which number is the best estimate of the number of meals the restaurant served for lunch that day rounded to the nearest 10?

    A. 280   **B.** 160

    C. 190   **D.** 310

3.OA.A.3

18. Karen has 45 slices of pizza left over from a party. She eats 3 slices and divides the rest among 7 containers. Which equation represents the number of slices in each container?

    A. $(45-3)\div 7=s$ **B.** $(45-3)-7=s$

    C. $(45+3)\div 7=s$ **D.** $(45-7)\div 3=s$

3.OA.D.8

19. Jacki draws this model to represent a fraction.

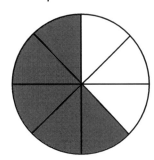

Which expression represents the shaded part of this model?

    A. $\frac{1}{3}+\frac{1}{3}+\frac{1}{3}$ **B.** $\frac{1}{5}+\frac{1}{5}+\frac{1}{5}$

    C. $\frac{1}{8}+\frac{1}{8}+\frac{1}{8}+\frac{1}{8}+\frac{1}{8}$ **D.** $\frac{3}{5}+\frac{3}{5}+\frac{3}{5}$

3.NF.A.1

prepaze

COMPREHENSIVE ASSESSMENTS

20. Dawn covers a figure with square units. Each square has an area of 1 square unit. What is the area of this figure?

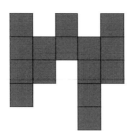

A. 20 square units
B. 18 square units
C. 16 square units
D. 15 square units

3.MD.C.5.B

21. Which is a better unit to use for the volume of an eyedropper?

A. liter
B. milliliter
C. kilogram
D. gram

3.MD.A.2

22. Look at this picture graph. How many votes did Demyan's pumpkin get?

Pumpkin Carving Competition	
Peter	🎃
Lynn	🎃
Demyan	🎃 🎃
Trent	🎃 🎃 🎃
Conrad	🎃 🎃 🎃 🎃

🎃 = 10 votes
🎃 = 5 votes

A. 20 votes
B. 40 votes
C. 15 votes
D. 30 votes

3.MD.B.3

COMPREHENSIVE ASSESSMENTS

23. What is the related addition equation for the phrase "5 groups of 8"?

    A. $5+5+5+5+5 =$ **B.** $8+8+8+8+8 =$

    C. $8+8+8+8 =$ **D.** $5+5+5+5+5+5+5 =$

                                                    (3.OA.A.1)

24. Complete the inequality.

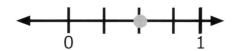

$$\frac{6}{10} < \underline{\hspace{3cm}}$$

    A. $\frac{5}{10}$ **B.** $\frac{4}{10}$ **C.** $\frac{3}{10}$ **D.** $\frac{7}{10}$

                                                    (3.NF.A.3.D)

25. Which fraction is represented by the point on this number line?

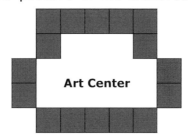

    A. $\frac{3}{1}$ **B.** $\frac{2}{4}$ **C.** $\frac{3}{4}$ **D.** $\frac{2}{1}$

                                                    (3.NF.A.2.B)

26. Mr. Ingram draws this picture of his classroom art center.

Art Center

The art center is surrounded by desks which have an area of 1 square foot. What is the area of the art center in square feet?

    A. 13 square feet   **B.** 15 square feet

    C. 20 square feet   **D.** 18 square feet

                                                    (3.MD.C.6)

prepaze

COMPREHENSIVE ASSESSMENTS

27. What is the area of the rectangle?

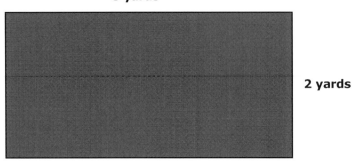

5 yards

2 yards

A. 15 square yards **B.** 10 square yards
C. 28 square yards **D.** 14 square yards

3.MD.C.7

28. Look at this picture graph. How many books did Caleb read?

Reading Competition	
Asher	📕
Cassidy	📕
Nathan	📕📕📕📕📕
Caleb	📕📕📕📕
Flynn	📕
Emile	📕📕📕

📕 = 1 book

A. 1 book   **B.** 5 books   **C.** 3 books   **D.** 4 books

3.MD.B.3

NAME: .... DATE: ....

193

COMPREHENSIVE ASSESSMENTS

29. What is the perimeter of the shape?

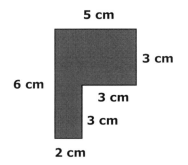

5 cm
3 cm
6 cm
3 cm
3 cm
2 cm

A. 22 cm   **B.** 26 cm

C. 12 cm   **D.** 30 cm

(3.MD.D.8)

30. Model this expression on the number line.

$$324 - 165 + 92$$

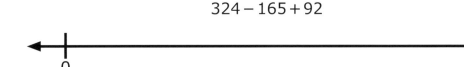

0

(3.NBT.A.2)

31. The sides of a square-shaped room are 4 yards long. Amy wants to buy carpet to cover the floor of the room. If the carpet costs $10.00 per square yard, how much will it cost to buy enough carpet for the room?

_____

(3.MD.D.8)

32. Draw two arrays to represent this expression: 4(3+7).

(3.OA.B.5)

prepaze

COMPREHENSIVE ASSESSMENTS

33. In gym class, the children get into groups of 5 to play a ball game. If there are 15 boys and 25 girls, how many teams are there?

_____

3.OA.A.2

34. Kara is baking cupcakes and has a bag of 54 chocolate chips. If she wants to put the same number of chocolate chips in each of the 9 cupcakes, how many chocolate chips need to go into each cupcake?

A. Write a multiplication equation that can be used to solve: _____

B. Write a division equation that can be used to solve: _____

C. Answer: _____

3.OA.A.4

35. What is the length of this hotdog to the nearest quarter inch?

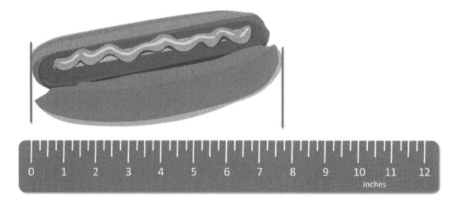

_____

3.MD.B.4

COMPREHENSIVE ASSESSMENTS

36. How many pairs of opposite sides are parallel?

_____ pairs.

3.G.A.1

37. Model the division statement $20 \div 5$.

3.OA.A.2

38. Zane believes this model represents $\frac{1}{5}$. Do you agree with Zane? Explain your reasoning.

_____

_____

_____

3.G.A.2

prepaze

COMPREHENSIVE ASSESSMENTS

39. A square mirror has sides that are 6 feet long. What is the mirror's area?

_____ square feet

3.MD.C.7

40. Will an even number times an even number always result in an even number or an odd number? Explain your reasoning.

_____

_____

_____

3.OA.D.9

41. Write an equation that represents another way to find the value of this equation: $54 \div 9 =$

_____

3.OA.D.9

42. Bill uses this model to prove $\frac{1}{3}$ is greater than $\frac{5}{7}$.

$\frac{1}{3}$ 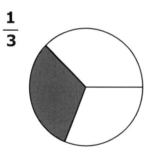 $\frac{5}{7}$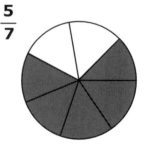

Do you agree with Bill? Explain your reasoning.

_____

_____

_____

3.G.A.2

COMPREHENSIVE ASSESSMENTS

43. Arthur can either work 6 hours a week for $9 an hour at the coffee shop or he can work for 7 hours a week for $8 an hour at the bookstore. Where will he make the most money in one week, the bookstore or the coffee shop?

_____

_____

_____

3.OA.C.7

44. Oscar believes the area of the orange shape is 16 square units. Each square has an area of 1 square unit. Do you agree with Oscar? Explain your reasoning.

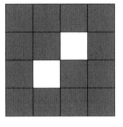

_____

_____

_____

3.MD.C.7

45. How many pairs of opposite sides are parallel?

_____

3.G.A.1

prepaze

ANSWERS AND EXPLANATIONS

prepaze

www.prepaze.com

OPERATIONS AND ALGEBRAIC THINKING
UNIT 1: GROUPING

1   Answer: D
Explanation: Count the number of apples in each group. There are 4 apples in each group, so you can add $4+4+4$ to count the total number of apples.

2   Answer: A
Explanation: To find how many Haumea days are equal to 3 Earth days, you must first do $24 \div 4 = 6$, then $6 \times 3 = 18$.

3   Answer: C
Explanation: Each of the bothers get 4 pancakes, and there are 12 pancakes in total. So, there are $12 \div 4 = 3$ brothers, and each will need one plate.

4   Answer: D
Explanation: To find the number of bikes in each group, you could use the equation $20 \div 4 = 5$.

5   Answer: C
Explanation: $3 \times 4 = 12$, count four 3 times: $4+4+4=12$.

6   Answer: B
Explanation: To find the total number of pens he has, you could use the equation $15 \times 5 = 75$.

7   Answer: A
Explanation: The equation $11+8+12=c$ can be used to find the total number of crickets the frog ate.

8   Answer: D
Explanation: To find the number of cards each player gets, you must do $36 \div 6 = 6$ which means each person gets 6 cards.

9   Answer: C
Explanation: There are 15 total flowers and 3 planters. To find the number of flowers in each planter, you must do $15 \div 3 = 5$.

10   Answer: B
Explanation: To find the number of legs the spiders have all together, you must do $5 \times 8 = 40$ which means the spiders have 40 legs all together.

11   Answer: B
Explanation: 4 boxes of 8 pencils is the same as 4 groups of 8 pencils or counting eight 4 times so $4 \times 8 = 32$

12   Answer: A
Explanation: First, to find the total number of books, you must do $19+23=42$. Then to find the number of books on each shelf, you must do $42 \div 6 = 7$.

13   Answer: No, he is incorrect.
Explanation: The model shows $2+2+2+3$ because there are 3 stars in the last group. This model cannot be used for a multiplication model or repeated addition model because it does not have equal groups. The model would have to show 4 groups with 2 stars in each group – not 3 stars in the last group.

14   Answer: $24 \div 8 = 3$ or $24 \div 3 = 8$
Explanation: There are 8 equal groups of 24 balloons in total. To find the number of balloons in each group, you must do $24 \div 8 = 3$.

15   Answer: 9 bags
Explanation: First find the total weight by adding 56 and 16. $56+16=72$. Then since she puts 8 ounces in each bag, divide 72 with 8. So you will get $72 \div 8 = 9$ bags.

16   Answer: 7 nights
Explanation: After the first night, there were 84 pages left. If Anna reads 12 pages each night, it will take 7 more nights because $84 \div 12 = 7$.

17   Answer: Cameron
Explanation: Cameron bought 4 packs of gum with 7 pieces in each so think of this as 4 groups of 7, which is $4 \times 7 = 28$. Julie

bought 5 packs of gum with 5 pieces in each pack so think of this as 5 groups of 5 or $5 \times 5 = 25$. Using the inequality $28 > 25$ to compare the amounts, Cameron bought more gum.

18 Answer: 7 people
Explanation: To find the amount of people at the part, you must do $21 \div 3 = 7$.

19 Answer: The array should show 5 rows of 8 = 40 cupcakes
Explanation: 2 rows of 8 and 3 rows of 8 is the same as 5 rows of 8 because 2 rows + 3 rows = 5 rows. 5 rows of 8 is the same as counting 8 five times or $5 \times 8 = 40$.

20 Answer: Answers may vary
Explanation: The word problem needs to have 2 groups of 8 to fit the equation $2 \times 8 = 16$.

OPERATIONS AND ALGEBRAIC THINKING UNIT 2: PROPERTIES OF MULTIPLICATION AND DIVISION

1 Answer: C
Explanation: The number line shows 3 jumps of 3 so the missing factor is 3 because $3 \times 3 = 9$.

2 Answer: B
Explanation: $4 \times n = 24$ can be used to solve the problem. There are 24 chairs divided into 4 groups or $24 \div 4$. Think 4 groups of what number = 24? $4 \times 6 = 24$ so $24 \div 4 = 6$, there will be 6 chairs at each table.

3 Answer: B
Explanation: Associative Property of multiplication states that when three or more numbers are multiplied, the product is the same regardless of the grouping of the factors. So, $3 \times (2 \times 8) = (3 \times 2) \times 8$.

4 Answer: A
Explanation: Twice as many means multiply by 2 or double the number. So, you can solve by multiplying 15 and 2.

5 Answer: D
Explanation: Separating 63 balls into equal groups can be represented by the division expression.

6 Answer: C
Explanation: The distributive property lets you find a sum by multiplying each addend separately and then add the products. So, to find a solution for $2(1 + 3)$, you can multiply 2×1 and 2×3 then add them together.

7 Answer: D
Explanation: 35 pencils divided into 7 boxes equals 5 pencils in each box because $35 \div 7 = 5$ or $7 \times 5 = 35$.

8 Answer: A
Explanation: Using distributive property of multiplication $5 \times (6 + 1)$ can be written as $(5 + 6) + (5 + 1)$.

9 Answer: C
Explanation: 16 stars divided into groups of 4 equals 4 stars in each group because $16 \div 4 = 4$ or $4 \times 4 = 16$

10 Answer: A
Explanation: 4 groups of the same number are the same as 36 means 4 groups of what = 36. Think $4 \times n = 36$ or 4 groups of $9 = 36$.

11 Answer: D
Explanation: The commutative property of multiplication states that you can multiply numbers in any order. So, 3×6 is the same as 6×3.

12 Answer: B
Explanation: To solve $6 \times n = 30$ think of the related division equation $30 \div 6 = n$ or count 6 until you reach 30, which would be 5 times.

13 Answer: A. $22
**   B. Answers may vary**
Explanation: 3 bags of apples for $4 each is the same as counting 3 groups of 4 or $3 \times 4 = 12$. 2 melons for $5 each is the same

as counting 2 groups of 5 or $2 \times 5 = 10$. Add $\$10 + \$12 = \$22$ spent at the store.

14   Answer: 24 apples
Explanation: Charlie draws 6 rows of 4 which means there are 6×4 or 24 apples.

15   Answer: Answers may vary
Explanation: The word problem needs to show 7 groups of a number equaling 63, 63 divided into 7 groups, 63 divided into groups of 7, or 9 groups of $7 = 63$.

16   Answer: 5 and 10
Explanation: The missing values should cause each expression to have a value of 15.

17   Answer: Yes, Samantha is correct.
Explanation: $49 \div 7 = n$ is the same as $n \times 7 = 49$ because 49 divided into 7 groups equals 7 in each group and $7 \times 7 = 49$. 7 groups with 7 in each group are the factors in the multiplication equation. Instead of dividing 49 into 7 groups, with 7 in each group, you can multiply and count the repeated groups as 7 groups of 7 ($7 \times 7 = 49$). The total amount 49 does not change whether it is written as a multiplication or division equation.

18   Answer: 9
Explanation: No matter how the numbers are grouped, they can be multiplied.

19   Answer: Array should have 4 rows of 10 or 10 rows of 4
Explanation: The expression is equivalent to $4(10)$ or 40. This can be determined using the distributive property.

20   Answer: They are both correct
Explanation: To solve $n = 6 \times 8$, you can think of this as 6 groups of 8, 8 groups of 6, counting 6 eight times or counting 8 six times because $8 \times 6 = 48$ and $6 \times 8 = 48$.

> **OPERATIONS AND ALGEBRAIC THINKING**
> **UNIT 3: MULTIPLY AND DIVIDE WITHIN 100**

1   Answer: C
Explanation: 6 fours are the same as 4 written 6 times ($4 + 4 + 4 + 4 + 4 + 4$) or 6 groups of 4, which is the same as 6×4

2   Answer: D
Explanation: 23 rounds to 20 18 rounds to 20 20 baseball cards + 20 basketball cards = 40 cards 40 cards $\div 4$ = ABOUT 10 cards in each box

3   Answer: C
Explanation: $7 \times 8 = 56$, which is not enough to buy the $\$60$ video game. $7 \times 9 = 63$, which is enough to buy the $\$60$ video game, with $\$3$ left over.

4   Answer: D
Explanation: 5 is always a factor of a $2 -$ digit number ending in 5. Because 5 times any number will result in a product that ends in 5 or 0. $5 \times 7 = 35 / 85 \div 5 = 17$

5   Answer: B
Explanation: Counting 20 five – dollar bills is the same as counting 20 groups of 5 or 20×5

6   Answer: C
Explanation: The first expression (6×5) represents the total number of books Kalida starts with, she then gives away 12 books (-12) and receives 3 more books ($+3$).

7   Answer: C
Explanation: 6×8 is the same as (6×5) + (6×3) because 8 can be split into two addends $5 + 3$, multiply each by 6 and then add the products together to get the final product.

8   Answer: D
Explanation: Add 4 degrees to 75 since the temperature started at 75 degrees and rose 4 degrees. $75 + 4 = 79$ degrees. Then subtract

79 – 68 to find the difference in the afternoon and nighttime temperature.

9 Answer: B
Explanation: Gavin works for 6 days earning $8 a day, multiply to find the amount of money he made: $6 \times 8 = \$48$. The sneakers cost $56 so subtract to find the amount of money he needs to buy the shoes: $56 - 48 = \$8$. If he saves $8 a day and he needs 8 more dollars, the he needs to save for 1 more day.

10 Answer: B
Explanation: multiply by 2 $3 \times 2 = 6$ $6 \times 2 = 12$ $12 \times 2 = 24$.

11 Answer: C
Explanation: $8 \times 5 = 40$ and the product in the original problem is 48. To get from 40 to 48 add another group of 8, which is $8 \times 6 = 48$. $6 \times 8 = 48$ is the related multiplication fact for $48 \div 8 = 6$.

12 Answer: C
Explanation: Another way to solve 7×6 is to break 6 into $3 + 3$, $7 \times 3 = 21$ and $7 \times 3 = 21$ so add $21 + 21 = 42$, which is the same as $7 \times 6 = 42$.

13 Answer: A
Explanation: $81 is the total amount of money spent, each plant costs $9 so divide to find the number of plants $81 \div 9 = 9$.

14 Answer: B
Explanation: Gerald can multiply 9×9 which is one more group of 9 than 8×9. Then subtract one group of 9 to get the same answer as 8×9. 9×9 and subtract one group of 9 $9 \times 9 = 81 - 9 = 72$ $8 \times 9 = 72$.

15 Answer: Yes
Explanation: Yes, a number that is 6 is also divisible by 3 because 6 is a multiple of 3 and 3 is a factor of 6 so if one number can be divided by 6, like $36 \div 6$, it can also be divided by 3: $36 \div 3$.

16 Answer: Answers may vary
Explanation: The first step in the word problem must be adding $16 + 29$. Then subtract 18. Sample: Jerry got $16 from his grandpa and then mowed a lawn for $29. Then he spent $18 on a new game. How much money does he have left?

17 Answer: A. 9 boxes
B. Yes, she will have 7 cookies left over
Explanation: Each box comes with 8 cookies. Jane needs to buy 9 boxes because $8 \times 9 = 72$ cookies. If she buys 8 boxes: that would be $8 \times 8 = 64$ cookies and that is not enough because she needs 65 cookies. Yes, she will have 7 cookies left over because $72 - 65 = 7$.

18 Answer: An odd number
Explanation: An odd number times an odd number will result in an odd number. Think of the array for 5×3, there are 5 rows of 3 in each row, so the total will be odd because there is an odd number of rows with an odd number in each row.

19 Answer: Answers may vary
Explanation: 36 divided into 3 groups equals 12 in each group.

20 Answer: $(65 - 5) \div 5 = \$12$ a day for lunch
Explanation: She started with $65 and had $5 now. Subtract to find the amount of money she spent. $65 - 5 = \$60$. If she spent 60 over 5 days, divide to find how much money she spent each day $60 \div 5 = 12$, she spends $12 each day for lunch.

OPERATIONS AND ALGEBRAIC THINKING
CHAPTER REVIEW

1 Answer: C
Explanation: To find the total number of milk cans he delivered in a week, you must do $12 \times 4 = 48$.

2   Answer: A

Explanation: There are 4 columns and 3 rows.

3   Answer: D

Explanation: To find how many flowers do you put in each vase, you can use the equation $16 \div 4 = 4$.

4   Answer: D

Explanation: If each tent can sleep 3 people and 18 people are going camping, think $? \times 3 = 18$. Use the diagram and circle groups of 3 to represents the 3 people in a tent. 6 groups of 3 people = 18 people total. $6 \times 3 = 18$ so they need 6 tents for everyone to sleep.

5   Answer: B

Explanation: Count the number of apples in each group. There are 4 apples in each group, so you can add $4 + 4 + 4$ to count the total number of apples.

6   Answer: D

Explanation: Each hour, Logan is paid $\$8$ and he works 10 hours, which is the same as counting 10 groups of 8 or $10 \times 8 = 80$.

7   Answer: B

Explanation: 4 bags with 8 apples in each bag = $4 \times 8 = 32$ red apples, 3 bags with 6 green apples = $3 \times 6 = 18$ green apples. So, the total apple is $32 + 18 = 50$.

8   Answer: C

Explanation: To find the number of friends she has, you must do $20 \div 5 = 4$.

9   Answer: A

Explanation: A 2-digit number that ends in zero is always divisible by 10 because 10 times any whole number results in a number ending in zero. $50 \div 10 = 5$, $10 \times 345 = 3,450$.

10   Answer: C

Explanation: The 2 is being distributed to the $(7+13)$.

11   Answer: A

Explanation: Think $8 \times n = 56$ or $56 \div 8 = 7$ because the cups come 8 in a pack so think how many groups of 8 are needed to get 56 cups? $8 \times 7 = 56$.

12   Answer: B

Explanation: The answer to a division problem is called a quotient.

13   Answer: B

Explanation: 12 stickers split into 4 groups means $12 \div 4 = 3$. The model needs to show 4 groups since the problem is dividing 12 stickers into 4 groups.

14   Answer: D

Explanation: $8 \times 2 = 16$, if you double 16 $(16 + 16 = 32)$, that is the same as multiplying 8×4 $(=32)$. You can double 8x2 because 4 is twice as much as 2 so you can count 8 two times (8, 16) and then double 16 $(16 + 16)$ which is the same as counting 8 four times or 8×4.

15   Answer: C

Explanation: The equation $\frac{48}{8} =$ would help us find out how many days Irene did push-ups.

16   Answer: C

Explanation: Associative Property of multiplication states that when three or more numbers are multiplied, the product is the same regardless of the grouping of the factors. So, $2 \times (8 \times 5) = (2 \times 8) \times 5$.

17   Answer: B

Explanation: A number that is divisible by 4 will always be divisible by 2 because 4 is twice as much as 2. $(2 \times 2 = 4$, so any number that can be divided by 4 can also be divided by 2. They are both even numbers, so they will both be divided into even groups.

18   Answer: C

Explanation: Casey spent $\$18$ because he bought 9 chocolate bars that cost $\$2$ each. Think of this as 9 groups of 2 or $9 \times 2 = 18$.

19   Answer: C
Explanation: To solve $56 \div 8 = n$, think $8 \times n = 56$ because 56 divided into 8 groups is the same as thinking 8 groups of some number equals 56.

20   Answer: D
Explanation: First, you must add $24 + 6 + 30 = 60$ to find the total number of strings. Then you must divide $60 \div 10 = 6$. To find the number of friends she will be able to give the bracelets to.

OPERATIONS AND ALGEBRAIC THINKING EXTRA PRACTICE

1   Answer: D
Explanation: 32 shells split into 4 bags is the same as $32 \div 4 = n$. Use the related multiplication equation to solve for the unknown factor: $4 \times n = 32$, $4 \times 8 = 32$, $32 \div 4 = 8$ so the unknown factor is 8. There are 8 shells in each bag.

2   Answer: B
Explanation: $35 \div 5 = 7$ matches the diagram because the total amount represented is 35 which is divided into 5 groups, with 7 in each group.

3   Answer: A
Explanation: Mrs. Jones has 30 pieces of candy total. She is using 5 pieces in each bag so think 30 pieces divided into 5 in a group = how many groups? $30 \div 5 = n$ OR think of this as multiplication: 5 pieces of candy in each bag $\times$ the number of bags = 30 so the correct equations to solve are $30 \div 5 = n$; $5 \times n = 30$.

4   Answer: D
Explanation: $100 \div 5 = 20$, $100 \div 4 = 25$, and $100 \div 2 = 50$.

5   Answer: B
Explanation: 2 rows + 4 rows = 6 rows; 6 rows $\times$ 6 equals 36.

6   Answer: B
Explanation: First, add the money she made $15 + 28 = \$43$, then subtract the money she spent $43 - 14 = \$29$.

7   Answer: A
Explanation: First, you have to find the total number of muffins, which is $3 \times 10 = 30$. Then you have to subtract the number eaten to find the total, which is $30 - 2 = 28$. Then, to find the number Ashley shared with each of her friends, you must do $28 \div 7 = 4$.

8   Answer: B
Explanation: $8 \times n = 48$ or $48 \div 8 = n$. If there are 48 legs total and Gary drew 8 legs on each spider, think $8 \times$ what number $= 48$.

9   Answer: C
Explanation: $(50 - 14) \div 4$ First, subtract to find the number of pages remaining. $50 - 14$, then divide by 4 to find how many pages she needs to read each day.

10   Answer: Maria
Explanation: Carlos has 40 books because 5 groups of 8 is $5 \times 8 = 40$. Maria has 42 books because 6 stacks of 7 is $6 \times 7 = 42$. So, Maria has more books.

11   Answer: $(8 \div 2) \times 8 = 32$ pepperoni slices
Explanation: Half of the pizza means divide by 2. $(8 \div 2)$, then multiply the number of pizzas times the number of slices in each pizza $(8 \div 2) \times 8 = 32$ pepperoni slices.

12   Answer: The bookstore
Explanation: Coffee Shop: 6 hours a week for $9 an hour is $6 \times 9 = \$54$ a week Bookstore: 7 hours a week for $8 an hour is $7 \times 8 = \$56$ a week.

13   Answer: The picture should be 5 groups with 9 circles or markings in each group. $5 \times 9 = 45$ beads
Explanation: Each bracelet needs 9 beads and is making 5 bracelets so think of this as 5 groups of 9 or 5×9. The picture needs to model 5 groups with 9 circles in each group.

14   **Answer: An even number times an odd number will result in an even number.**

Explanation: Think of the array 5×6: there are 5 rows with 6 in each row. Because one factor is even, you can pair off the dots in the array since there is an even number of dots in each row.

15   **Answer: 9 bags**

Explanation: To find the number of jelly bean bags made, you could use the equation $(56+16) \div 8 = 9$ which means 9 bags were made.

16   **Answer: $125 - (9 \times 10) = \$35$ for lunch**

Explanation: $125 - (9 \times 10) = \$35$ for lunch If each ticket costs $9 and there are 10 people going to the movies, multiply 9×10 to find the cost of the tickets $90. Subtract $125 - 90$ to find the amount of money that was used for lunch, $35.

17   **Answer: Each notebook cost $4**

Explanation: First, find the amount of money Georgina spent on the books by subtracting the change from the amount of money she had: $30 - 2 = \$28$ so the books cost $28. Then divide $28 \div 7$ to find how much each book cost or think $7 \times n = 28$. Each book cost $4.

18   **Answer: A. $4 \times 7 = 28$ or $7 \times 4 = 28$**
    B. $28 \div 4 = 7$ or $28 \div 7 = 4$
    7 or 4 28 4 or 7
    C. 7 or 4   D. 28
    E. 4 or 7

Explanation: The number line shows 4 groups of 7 or 4 jumps of 7.

19   **Answer: Answers may vary**

Explanation: The word problem needs to have 2 groups of 8 to fit the equation $2 \times 8 = 16$.

20   **Answer: 6 crackers**

Explanation: To find the number of crackers left, first you must find $15 - 3 = 12$. Then you must find the number of crackers each friend will get, which is $12 \div 2 = 6$.

NUMBER & OPERATIONS IN BASE TEN
UNIT 1: PLACE VALUE ROUNDING

1   **Answer: B**
Explanation: 112 can be rounded to 110.

2   **Answer: D**
Explanation: 217 rounded to the nearest hundred is 200.

3   **Answer: A**
Explanation: 175 rounded to the nearest 10 is 180.

4   **Answer: C**
Explanation: The farmer harvests between 400 and 500 strawberries, so the number must be less than 500 but close to it.

5   **Answer: C**
Explanation: The number of acorns is between 200 and 300 but rounded to the nearest ten must be 200.

6   **Answer: D**
Explanation: $43 \approx 40$ and $29 \approx 30$ so $40 + 30 = 70$ so James has about 70 coins.

7   **Answer: B**
Explanation: 17 is closer to 0 than 100.

8   **Answer: C**
Explanation: 125 can be rounded to 130.

9   **Answer: A**
Explanation: 704 rounded to the nearest ten is 700.

10   **Answer: B**
Explanation: 1,031 can be rounded to the nearest 1,000.

11   **Answer: D**
Explanation: 39 can be rounded to 40, 28 can be rounded to 30 and 21 can be rounded to 20. 39 can be rounded to 40, 28 can be rounded to 30 and 21 can be rounded to 20. Adding 40, 30 and 20, the answer is 90.

12 Answer: B

Explanation: The number 1,025 rounded to the nearest hundred is 1,000.

13 Answer: 310 star stickers

Explanation: 311 can be rounded to 310.

14 Answer: 280 animal stickers

Explanation: 284 can be rounded to 280.

15 Answer: 4,000

Explanation: 3,995 rounded to the nearest hundred is 4,000.

16 Answer: 100 stickers

Explanation: 74 rounded to the nearest hundred is 100.

17 Answer: Answers may vary

Explanation: Sarah could have between 25 and 35 stickers. If Isaiah has 10 fewer stickers, he could have between 15 and 25 stickers.

18 Answer: 120 pickup trucks

Explanation: 121 can be rounded to 120.

19 Answer: 210 cars

Explanation: 206 can be rounded to 210.

20 Answer: 200 minivans

Explanation: 185 can be rounded to 200 when rounded to the nearest hundred.

NUMBER & OPERATIONS IN BASE TEN
UNIT 2: ADD AND SUBTRACT WITHIN 1000

1 Answer: B

Explanation: Student uses understanding of the standard algorithm to regroup tens and ones.

2 Answer: C

Explanation: Student demonstrates an understanding of the equal sign as a symbol showing both expressions should have the same value. $851 + 109 - 487 = 473$. $473 - 145 = 328$.

3 Answer: A

Explanation: Student uses the associative property to show the number of candies eaten by both sisters and subtracts the amount of candy eaten by Ronaldo. The equation will be $200 - 50 - 50 - 10$ which is same as $200 - (50+50) - 10$.

4 Answer: C

Explanation: Student reads the graph correctly and adds $160 + 220 + 240 + 160 = 780$.

5 Answer: A

Explanation: Student uses place value understanding to determine the difference. $1000 - 789 = 211$.

6 Answer: B

Explanation: 630 is on both sides of the equation. Since both 630 $+ 320 = 950$, both expressions will have a value of 950.

7 Answer: B

Explanation: The student understands the properties of operations can be used to simplify expressions.

8 Answer: C

Explanation: The student understands the properties of operations can be used to simplify expressions. To subtract 205 from 546, the students can first subtract from 546 and then subtract 5.

9 Answer: Answers may vary

Explanation: The student should use subtraction and addition to solve the problem; first determining the number of pages left to read with subtraction, then combining the values with addition. $238 - 111 = 127$. Liam read 127 pages. $238 - 182 = 56$. Sophia read 56 pages.

10 Answer: 725

Explanation: The student should use subtraction and addition to solve this multistep problem. The number written in the journal is 538. Adding 187 to this number will yield the result 725.

11   Answer: 240

Explanation: The student may use strategies based on place value and the properties of operations to group numbers in different ways. $109 + 315 + 287 - 471 = 240$.

12   Answer: 171

Explanation: The student may use strategies based on place value and the properties of operations to group numbers in different ways. $628 - 1000 + 746 - 203 = 171$.

13   Answer: a – the second box;
**   b – the second box has 180**
**   calculators and the third**
**   box has 90 calculators;**
**   c – 400 calculators**

Explanation: The student should first determine the box with the greatest number of calculators. The second box has a greater number of calculators than the first box because it contains "twice as many". The values for the second and third box should then be compared to the value of the first box. The student may use a variety of strategies, including guess and check or writing an equation to determine the total number of calculators in each box. c – The student should add 130 and 270 (or they may add 130, 180, and 90) to determine the total number of calculators. If using the standard algorithm, the student should regroup the tens when adding.

14   Answer:

Explanation: When modeling the sum of 105 and 585 on a number line, the student should create a drawing where the "jumps" are the correct (appropriate) size.

15   Answer:

Explanation: When modeling the operations (addition and subtraction) on a number line, the student should create a drawing where the "jumps" are the correct (appropriate) size.

16   Answer: 160

Explanation: Student may use a variety of addition and subtraction strategies to determine how many more miles. The student may also notice that the bar that represents the number of miles in February and September are the same height and may then recognize they only need to subtract the number of miles in August and January. $240 - 80 = 160$.

17   Answer: 142

Explanation: Student should recognize how to regroup with zeroes when subtracting the two numbers represented by Model A and Model B. $630 - 488 = 142$.

18   Answer: Answers may vary.
**   The Airbus A380 will carry more**
**   travelers.**

Explanation: The student may use strategies of addition and/or subtraction to determine the total number of travelers for the 3 airplanes, and then must compare the values. Airbus A320 and Boeing 727 will carry a total of $220 + 189 + 220 + 189 = 818$ passengers on roundtrips. Airbus A380 will carry a total of $495 + 495 = 990$ passengers on a round trip. Airbus A380 will carry more passengers.

19   Answer: Answers may vary. Possible
**   response may include regrouping**
**   the 15 ones as 1 ten and 5 ones.**

Explanation: The student should recognize the 15 ones can be regrouped as 1 ten and 5 ones, which will change the value of the result to 985.

20   Answer: Answers may vary. Possible
**   response may include regrouping**
**   the values in each place.**

Explanation: The student should recognize the value of each digit in the number 715 can be regrouped for subtraction using the standard algorithm. By correcting the regrouping mistake, the answer can be found as $715 - 686 = 29$.

NUMBER & OPERATIONS IN BASE TEN
UNIT 3: MULTIPLY BY 10

1 Answer: B
Explanation: 2 tens are the same as 2 groups of 10. 2 groups of 10 or $2 \times 10 = 20$. Repeated addition $10 + 10 = 20$.

2 Answer: C
Explanation: 4 $10 bills are the same as 4 groups of 10 or $4 \times 10 = 40$. Count repeated groups: $10 + 10 + 10 + 10 = 40$.

3 Answer: B
Explanation: 6×10 is the same as 6 group of 10 or 6 plates with 10 cookies on each plate.

4 Answer: C
Explanation: 4 buses with 20 people in each bus $= 4 \times 20 = 80$. Or count repeated groups $20 + 20 + 20 + 20 = 80$.

5 Answer: A
Explanation: 5 ten-dollar bills equal $50. If Kristian shares the $50 with 5 friends, they will each get $10 because $10 \times 5 = 50$.

6 Answer: C
Explanation: 3 tens are equal to 30 because $3 \times 10 = 30$. 1 ten is equal to 10. 5 tens are equal to 50 because $5 \times 10 = 50$. $30 + $10 + $50 = 90$.

7 Answer: D
Explanation: 4×5 tens are the same as 4×50 because 5 tens or 5 groups of 10 is 50. $4 \times 50 = 200$.

8 Answer: B

Explanation: 6 packs of 30 plates is the same as $6 \times 30 = 180$. $6 \times 3 = 18$ so $6 \times 30 = 180$.

9 Answer: A
Explanation: Ten 10s is the same as 10 groups of 10 or 10×10. Since Colby has ten $10 bills, $10 \times 10 = 100$.

10 Answer: C
Explanation: 6 packs of 50 nails is the same as counting 50 6 times or multiplying $50 \times 6 = 300$. Another way to solve is to break apart 50 into 10×5 then multiply by 6: $6 \times 5 \times 10 = 300$.

11 Answer: D
Explanation: The model shows 3 rows of 4 squares with 10 in each square. 4 squares with 10 in each square is the same as $4 \times 10 = 40$ so this model shows 3 rows with 40 in each row.

12 Answer: B
Explanation: If each hour is 60 minutes, then is 8 hours $\times$ 60 minutes in 1 hour $= 480$ minutes. Then add 15 minutes to 480 minutes. $480 + 15 = 495$ minutes.

13 Answer: A
Explanation: 40×8 is the same as $(4 \times 10) \times 8$ because $4 \times 10 = 40$ and $40 \times 8 = 40 \times 8$.

14 Answer: B
Explanation: First, subtract the amount the bag weighs from the total weight: $170 - 10 = 160$. Then divide 160 by 8 apples to find the weight of each apple or think $8 \times ? = 160$. $8 \times 20 = 160$.

15 Answer: D
Explanation: First, add the number of cans in each box: $14 + 16$, then multiply by 9 since he bought 9 boxes $= (14 + 16) \times 9$.

16 Answer: Answers may vary
Explanation: Roger solves 30×5 by using the equation 10×15. Break apart 30×5 into $(3 \times 5) \times 10$. $3 \times 5 = 15$ and then multiply by 10, $15 \times 10 = 150$ and $30 \times 5 = 150$.

17 Answer: A. 120
B. 480

Explanation: There are 20 rows with 6 seats in each row. So, there are $20 \times 6 = 120$ seats in one passenger car. In 4 passenger cars, there are $120 \times 4 = 480$ seats because 120×4 is same as $(12 \times 4) \times 10$ which is 480.

18 Answer: $10

Explanation: Peyton does not have enough money to buy the scooter because he has $7 \times \$40 = \$280$. The scooter costs $290. So Peyton would need $\$290 - \$280 = \$10$ more.

19 Answer: Yes

Explanation: Number of cookies in Sawyer's box: 10 boxes with 4 cookies in each box $= 10 \times 4 = 40$ cookies Number of cookies in Emily's box: 2 boxes of cookies with 2 bags of 10 cookies. 2 bags of $10 = 20$ cookies $\times$ 2 box.

20 Answer: 186 cards

Explanation: Possible list of steps. Find how many cards come in each pack by adding $37 + 3 = 40$ cards. She bought 5 packs of cards and so multiply to find the number of cards in the 5 packs: $5 \times 40 = 200$ cards. She lost 14 cards. So subtract 14: $200 - 14 = 186$ cards.

NUMBER & OPERATIONS IN BASE TEN CHAPTER REVIEW

1 Answer: B

Explanation: Using the standard algorithm, the first step in adding the numbers is to add the ones and regroup if necessary.

2 Answer: B

Explanation: 123 pages can be rounded to 100 and 276 pages can be rounded to 300. So, the estimated total pages is $100 + 300 = 400$.

3 Answer: D

Explanation: Using the standard algorithm, the first step would be subtracting 164

from 840 $(840 - 164)$ Subtraction is not commutative. As 4 can't be subtracted from 0, you will have to regroup 4 tens as 3 tens and 10 ones.

4 Answer: C

Explanation: The first step would involve subtracting 609 from 1,000. Subtraction is not commutative.

5 Answer: C

Explanation: Anna has about 20 pencils as 23 rounds to 20. Her mom gives her about 20 more pencils as 18 rounds to 20. She has about $20 + 20 = 40$ pencils.

6 Answer: B

Explanation: The missing side length of the park can be found by doing $145 - 60$. The distance around the park can be found by adding $175 + 145 + 175 + 145$.

7 Answer: C

Explanation: The first missing side length can be found by doing $218 + 109$. The second missing side length is equal to its opposite side which is 388 ft. The missing lengths are 388 ft. and 327 ft.

8 Answer: D

Explanation: $346 can be rounded to $300 and $567 can be rounded to $600. The total amount of money rounded to the nearest hundred is $900.

9 Answer: B

Explanation: Rounded to the nearest hundred, one person has 1,800 cows and another person has 4,000 cows. So, together they have $1800 + 4000 = 5800$ cows.

10 Answer: C

Explanation: 54 can be rounded to 50 and 27 can be rounded to 30. The total rounded to the nearest ten is $50 + 30 = 80$.

11 Answer: D

Explanation: 568 can be rounded to 600 and 426 can be rounded to 400. The total number of students, rounded to the nearest hundred is $600 + 400 = 1000$.

12 Answer: $75

Explanation: If the student make one part, 2 parts comes from company. So, $900 must be split into 3 equal parts. Each part is $300. So the students need to make $300. Since they already raised $225, they need to raise $300 − $225 = $75.

13 Answer: 1,200

Explanation: Rounding each value to the nearest hundred: 800 and 400. The total is 800 + 400 = 1200.

14 Answer: 500

Explanation: Rounding each value to the nearest ten: 370 and 130.

15 Answer: 1,800

Explanation: Each value rounded to the nearest hundred: 700, 300, and 800. The total is 700 + 300 + 800 = 1800.

16 Answer: 500

Explanation: Rounded to the nearest ten, she received approximately 500 flowers.

17 Answer: 423 + 125 − 275 = 273

Explanation: Add $125 he received from his father to his money $423. Then subtract the amount $275 he spends on a new game.

18 Answer: 400+100−250

Explanation: The line is split into 5 equal parts. Each part represents 100. Two down arrows goes in forward directions and one up arrow goes in reverse direction. The forward arrows represents 400 + 100. The reverse arrow represents 250.

19 Answer: 375+375- 600

Explanation: The line is split into 5 equal parts. Each part represents 150. Two down arrows goes in forward directions and one up arrow goes in reverse direction. The forward arrows represents 375 + 375. The reverse arrow represents 600.

20 Answer: 450 + 375 -600

Explanation: The line is split into 5 equal parts. Each part represents 150. Two down arrows goes in forward directions and one up arrow goes in reverse direction. The forward arrows represents 450 + 375. The reverse arrow represents 600.

NUMBER & OPERATIONS IN BASE TEN EXTRA PRACTICE

1 Answer: A

Explanation: There are 15 books on each shelf. And there are 4 shelves. So the total books are 15 × 4. 4 can be written as 2 × 2. So the equation can be written as 15 × 2 × 2 = 30 × 2.

2 Answer: C

Explanation: She watches TV for 45 × 6 minutes. It can be expressed as 90 × 3 as 6 can be split into 2 and 3 and 45 times 2 is 90.

3 Answer: A

Explanation: April has home work in 3 subjects and she spends 20 minutes for each subjects. She spends 60 minutes for completing her homework each day. She completes 60 minutes of homework for 2 days, which means she completes 120 minutes of homework.

4 Answer: A

Explanation: There are 2 boxes with 30 sheets, and 3 boxes with 40 sheets. The total is 180 sheets. 2 × 30 = 60 and 3 × 40 = 120. 60 + 120 = 180.

5 Answer: B

Explanation: Three boxes have 20 markers. 3 × 20 = 60 markers. 4 boxes have 10 markers. 4 × 10 = 40 markers. So he buys 60 + 40 = 100 markers in total.

6 Answer: A

Explanation: The total number of pages read is 34 + 79 + 54 = 167. She has to read 200 − 167 = 33 pages more.

7 Answer: D

Explanation: Tamir has 250 pennies, 40 quarters, and 8 half dollars.

8   Answer: A

Explanation: Using the strategy of halving and doubling, the expression 4×30 can be written as 2×60.

9   Answer: C

Explanation: The expression 30×4 represents the number of days in four months. Subtracting this value from 365 will determine the number of days in the remaining 7 months.

10   Answer: 12 hot dogs

Explanation: Jaren purchased 60 hot dogs (6×10) and used 48. So, she has $60 - 48 = 12$ hot dogs left.

11   Answer: 180 balloons

Explanation: Half of the packages is 6 packages. There are 30 balloons in each package, which means he purchased 180 balloons.

12   Answer: $70

Explanation: The class makes $350 by selling 50 tickets for $7each. $50 \times 7 = 350$. Their goal is $420. The difference is $420 - \$350 = \$70$.

13   Answer: Harry is correct

Explanation: Harry rounds 15 to the nearest ten: 20. He estimates he has 20 pencils per box; with 7 boxes this is approximately 140 pencils.

14   Answer: The expressions have the same value

Explanation: Both expressions have a value of 400.

15   Answer: 30 minutes

Explanation: If the amount of time is rounded to the nearest ten minutes, he exercises for 180 minutes. When you split or divide 180 into 6 equal groups, each group will get 30.

16   Answer: 20×6 30×4 40×3

Explanation: Each expression has a value of 120. You can use the multiplication facts for 12 to determine alternative expressions.

17   Answer: No, there is not enough information

Explanation: Landon's dog weighs approximately 20 pounds, which means if the estimate was made to the nearest ten pounds, the dog could weigh between 15 and 24 pounds.

18   Answer: $156

Explanation: Six people had $20 ($6 \times \$20 = \$120$ total) and they also each received $6 ($6 * \$6 = \$36$ total). The total amount of money is $\$120 + \$36 = \$156$.

19   Answer: 9,971

Explanation: When rounding to the nearest hundred, 9,971 will be 10,000.

20   Answer: Answers may vary

Explanation: Start by adding ones place. $7 + 4$ is 11. One ten from 11 will carry forward to tens place. Now add all tens place. Then add all hundreds place.

NUMBER & OPERATIONS - FRACTIONS
UNIT 1: UNDERSTANDING FRACTIONS

1   Answer: C

Explanation: The number line is divided into 3 equal size parts (thirds). The first hashmark after 0 on the number line represents $\frac{1}{3}$.

2   Answer: B

Explanation: 2 out of the 5 triangles are not shaded so $\frac{2}{5}$ is NOT shaded

3   Answer: B

Explanation: The ruler shows 1 inch divided into fourths. The paper clip covers 3 sections, or $\frac{3}{4}$ of an inch.

4   Answer: C

Explanation: Out of the 9 crayons, 4 are red. The question asks how many are not red, so subtract to find the remaining number of crayons that are not red: $9-4=5$ so 5 out of 9 are not red $=\frac{5}{9}$.

5 Answer: B

Explanation: The number line is divided into 2 equal parts (halves). The length between 0 and the first hash mark represents $\frac{1}{2}$ of a unit.

6 Answer: B

Explanation: The ruler shows 1 inch divided into sixths. The bug covers 5 sections, or $\frac{5}{6}$ of an inch.

7 Answer: A

Explanation: The number line is divided into sixths. The bar represents one-sixth.

8 Answer: D

Explanation: 8-foot-long piece of fabric is cut into 2-foot pieces. $8 \div 2$ is 4 so there are 4 pieces (2 foot long each). Since there are 4 pieces of fabric, each piece represents 1 out of 4 pieces or $\frac{1}{4}$.

9 Answer: C

Explanation: The number line is divided into 6 equal parts (sixths). The point on the number line represents $\frac{5}{6}$.

10 Answer: C

Explanation: $\frac{1}{2}$ of the model is shaded because 3 out of 6 parts are shaded and 3 is half of 6 $(3+3=6)$.

11 Answer: A

Explanation: Each fraction of a unit is represented by the space between hash marks. Number line A shows 8 spaces between 0 and 1.

12 Answer: C

Explanation: Sandra and her 4 sisters share the cake equally, so that is 5 people

sharing the cake (4 sisters and Sandra). Each person gets 1 out of the 5 pieces $=\frac{1}{5}$.

13 Answer: B

Explanation: The number line is divided into sixths. The grocery is located at $\frac{1}{6}$ and Isaiah's house is located at $\frac{5}{6}$. The distance between these values is $\frac{4}{6}$.

14 Answer: $\frac{2}{3}$

Explanation: The number line is divided into thirds. The fraction shown is $\frac{2}{3}$.

15 Answer: $\frac{1}{2}$

Explanation: The number line is divided into two equal parts. The point on the number line represents $\frac{1}{2}$.

16 Answer: No. The model should have 6 equal sized parts.

Explanation: The pieces in the circles are not equal so this does not show sixths. The circle needs to show 6 equal sized pieces to represent sixths.

17 Answer: Bethany is incorrect

Explanation: The ribbon ends at the 1-inch mark but does not start at 0. The length of the ribbon is $\frac{3}{4}$ inch.

18 Answer: The first hashmark

Explanation: The fraction $\frac{1}{3}$ is the first hashmark after zero on this number line.

19 Answer: Second Rectangle.

Explanation: Both rectangles are the same size. The first rectangle is divided into 8 equal parts. The second rectangle is divided into 5 equal parts, so each part is bigger than the first triangle parts.

20 Answer: The value of both points is the same.

Explanation: The number lines are divided into fourths, and the first hashmark after 0 represents $\frac{1}{4}$.

NUMBER & OPERATIONS - FRACTIONS
UNIT 2: EQUIVALENT FRACTIONS

1   Answer: C

Explanation: $\frac{3}{6}$ and $\frac{1}{2}$ are equivalent. You can simplify $\frac{3}{6}$ as $\frac{1}{2}$ by dividing 3 and 6 by 3.

2   Answer: C

Explanation: The ribbon is $\frac{3}{4}$ of the inch long. $\frac{3}{4}$ and $\frac{6}{8}$ are equivalent. You can multiply 3 and 4 by 2 to make $\frac{3}{4}$ as $\frac{6}{8}$.

3   Answer: A

Explanation: $\frac{1}{2}$ and $\frac{2}{4}$ are equivalent. You can multiply 1 and 2 by 2 to make $\frac{1}{2}$ as $\frac{2}{4}$.

4   Answer: B

Explanation: $\frac{3}{6}$ tiles are shaded. $\frac{3}{6}$ is same as $\frac{1}{2}$ because you can divide 3 and 6 by 3. Similarly $\frac{4}{8}$ can be simplified as $\frac{1}{2}$ by dividing 4 and 8 by 4.

5   Answer: D

Explanation: The shaded portion of the model is $\frac{4}{8}$, which is equivalent to $\frac{1}{2}$.

6   Answer: C

Explanation: The number line is divided into sixths. The distance between the Park and Mall is $\frac{2}{6}$. The fraction $\frac{1}{3}$ is equivalent to $\frac{2}{6}$.

7   Answer: A

Explanation: $\frac{6}{8}$ tiles are shaded. $\frac{6}{8}$ can be simplified into $\frac{3}{4}$ by dividing 6 and 8 by 2.

8   Answer: A

Explanation: The number line is divided into thirds. The distance between Sarah's House and the school is $\frac{2}{3}$ units. The fraction $\frac{4}{6}$ is equivalent to $\frac{2}{3}$.

9   Answer: D

Explanation: The shaded part of Model A is $\frac{6}{8}$. The fraction $\frac{3}{4}$ is equivalent to $\frac{6}{8}$.

10   Answer: C

Explanation: The fraction on the number line is $\frac{2}{6}$. Two-sixths is equivalent to $\frac{1}{3}$.

11   Answer: B

Explanation: The model in Response B shows $\frac{4}{6}$. The fraction $\frac{4}{6}$ is equivalent to $\frac{2}{3}$.

12   Answer: $\frac{3}{4}$

Explanation: The value of Point A is $\frac{6}{8}$. Additional fractions could be $\frac{12}{16}$, $\frac{24}{28}$. Since the standard 3.NF.A.3 emphasizes fractions with a denominator of 2, 3, 4, 6, or 8, most students will create $\frac{3}{4}$.

13   Answer: $\frac{3}{4}$ or $\frac{6}{8}$

Explanation: In the picture there are 4 squares. 2 of them are fully shaded. And 2 of them are shaded half. 2 half squares make one whole square. So, can say 3 squares are fully shaded.

14   Answer: $\frac{1}{2}$

Explanation: The value of Point A is $\frac{3}{6}$. Fractions equivalent to the value of Point A could include $\frac{2}{4}$ or $\frac{4}{8}$.

15   Answer: Answers may vary

Explanation: First mark $\frac{2}{8}$ on the first line and $\frac{1}{4}$ on the second line. You can see that the points are at a same distance from 0.

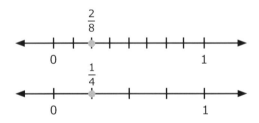

16   Answer: Yolanda is incorrect.

Explanation: The fraction bars cover 3 spaces in each number line, but the divisions on each number line are different.

17 Answer: Answers may vary

Explanation: Split the first rectangle into 3 equal parts and color the first part. Similarly, split the second rectangle into 6 equal parts and color the first 2 parts. You will notice that you have colored the same amount of space in both rectangles.

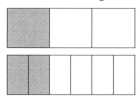

18 Answer: Penny is correct.

Explanation: The length modeled on Number Line A is $\frac{2}{4}$ and the length modeled on Number Line B is $\frac{4}{8}$. These fractions are equivalent.

19 Answer: The fractions are equivalent

Explanation: The fractions $\frac{4}{5}$ and $\frac{8}{10}$ have the same value.

20 Answer: They are the same distance.

Explanation: Riley walks $\frac{2}{3}$ miles to school, and John walks $\frac{4}{6}$ miles to school.

NUMBER & OPERATIONS - FRACTIONS
UNIT 3: COMPARE FRACTIONS

1 Answer: C

Explanation: A fraction represented as $\frac{a}{a}$, such as $\frac{4}{4}$, is the same as one whole.

2 Answer: C

Explanation: Students may want to find a common denominator, which would be eighths. In converting $\frac{2}{4}$ to eighths, the inequality compares $\frac{4}{8}$ and $\frac{5}{8}$. In comparing $\frac{4}{8}$ and $\frac{5}{8}$, $\frac{4}{8}$ is less. This means $\frac{2}{4}$ is less than $\frac{5}{8}$.

3 Answer: A

Explanation: The fraction $\frac{2}{1}$ is another way to represent the whole number 2. The fraction $\frac{3}{5}$ is less than 2.

4 Answer: B

Explanation: Students may choose the find a common denominator. In converting $\frac{3}{4}$ and $\frac{3}{6}$ to twelfths, the inequality compares $\frac{9}{12}$ and $\frac{6}{12}$. The fraction $\frac{9}{12}$ is greater than $\frac{6}{12}$. This means $\frac{3}{4}$ is greater than $\frac{3}{6}$. Another method may be recognizing $\frac{3}{4}$ is greater than $\frac{1}{2}$ and $\frac{3}{6}$ is equivalent to $\frac{1}{2}$.

5 Answer: C

Explanation: A whole number, a, can be represented by a fraction $\frac{a}{1}$.

6 Answer: A

Explanation: The fraction $\frac{1}{2}$ is equivalent to $\frac{2}{4}$. The fraction $\frac{2}{4}$ lies halfway between $\frac{1}{4}$ and $\frac{3}{4}$.

7 Answer: C

Explanation: Any number divided by 1 equals that number.

8 Answer: A

Explanation: The fraction $\frac{12}{2}$ is equivalent to 6. $\frac{6}{1}$ is also equals to 6.

9 Answer: B

Explanation: $\frac{10}{12}$ is a equivalent fraction for $\frac{5}{6}$. When you multiply both numerator and denominator in the fraction by 2, you will get $\frac{10}{12}$.

10 Answer:

Explanation: Fractions with a denominator of 1 are equivalent to whole numbers. The fraction $\frac{8}{1}$ is equivalent to 8.

prepaze

11   Answer: Soccer.

Explanation: $\frac{4}{6}$ is greater than $\frac{2}{6}$. So many students enjoy playing Soccer.

12   Answer: $\frac{2}{5} > \frac{2}{6}$

Explanation: Two parts are shaded in each model, but fifths are larger than sixths.

13   Answer: $\frac{3}{4} > \frac{3}{6}$

Explanation: The fraction $\frac{3}{4}$ is larger because fourths are larger than sixths.

14   Answer: $\frac{8}{8}$

Explanation: A whole is divided into 8 equal parts. The point A is marked on the whole. Fractions with the same numerator and denominator are equivalent to 1.

15   Answer: $\frac{4}{6} > \frac{4}{8}$

Explanation: The fraction $\frac{4}{6}$ is larger because sixths are larger than eighths.

16   Answer: $\frac{1}{8} < \frac{1}{6}$

Explanation: One part is shaded in each model, but sixths are larger than eighths.

17   Answer: Model B

Explanation: Fractions with the same numerator and denominator are equivalent to 1.

18   Answer: Jason is incorrect

Explanation: Two fractions are not equivalent because they have the same numerator. If the numerators are the same, the denominators must also be the same.

19   Answer: Breanna is incorrect.

Explanation: Two fractions are not equivalent because they have the same denominator. If the denominators are the same, the numerators must also be the same.

20   Answer: Model A

Explanation: Fractions with the same numerator and denominator are equivalent to 1.

NUMBER & OPERATIONS - FRACTIONS CHAPTER REVIEW

1   Answer: A

Explanation: The number line is divided into six equal segments between 0 and 1. These represents sixths.

2   Answer: A

Explanation: 3 out of the 8 pieces are colored so $\frac{3}{8}$ represents the colored part

3   Answer: B

Explanation: Out of the 7 days in a week, Carla goes to the gym twice. 2 out of 7 days represents Carla's time at the gym or $\frac{2}{7}$ of week Carla goes to the gym.

4   Answer: A

Explanation: The number line is divided into 3 equal segments between 0 and 1. This represents thirds. The distance between Point A and Point B is $\frac{2}{3}$.

5   Answer: B

Explanation: The number line is divided into halves. The length of the blue bar represents one half.

6   Answer: A

Explanation: Heather ate one out of 5 pieces or $\frac{1}{5}$. The remaining part is $\frac{4}{5}$ because there are 4 out of the 5 pieces left. $5 - 1 = 4$

7   Answer: A

Explanation: The number lines model two equivalent fractions.

8   Answer: D

Explanation: The point represents $\frac{1}{3}$.

9   Answer: B

Explanation: The fractions $\frac{3}{6}$ and $\frac{5}{8}$ are not equivalent. $\frac{5}{8}$ is greater than $\frac{3}{6}$.

10 Answer: A

Explanation: The fraction $\frac{2}{8}$ is equivalent to $\frac{1}{4}$.

11 Answer: $\frac{4}{6}$

Explanation: The number line is divided into sixths. The fraction shown is $\frac{4}{6}$.

12 Answer: $\frac{8}{8}$

Explanation: The model represents one whole. There are 8 parts and all of them are shaded.

13 Answer: $\frac{2}{4} = \frac{4}{8}$

Explanation: The fraction bars show how $\frac{2}{4}$ and $\frac{4}{8}$ are equivalent to $\frac{1}{2}$.

14 Answer: $\frac{3}{6}$

Explanation: The number line is divided into sixths; the distance between the park and Holden's house is $\frac{3}{6}$ mile.

15 Answer: $\frac{3}{4}$

Explanation: The number line is divided into four equal parts. The point on the number line represents $\frac{3}{4}$.

16 Answer: $\frac{2}{3} = \frac{4}{6}$

Explanation: The fraction bars show how $\frac{2}{3}$ and $\frac{4}{6}$ are equivalent.

17 Answer: $\frac{2}{4}, \frac{1}{2}, \frac{3}{6}$

Explanation: The fraction shown is $\frac{2}{4}$. Possible answers include $\frac{1}{2}, \frac{3}{6}, \frac{4}{8}, \frac{5}{10}$.

18 Answer: DeWayne is correct.

Explanation: The number line is divided into sixths. Each part has a value of $\frac{1}{6}$.

19 Answer: $\frac{6}{8}$

Explanation: The number line is divided into eight equal parts. The point on the number line represents.

20 Answer:

Explanation: Students may draw a number line model or a part whole model to show $\frac{3}{4}$ is the same as $\frac{6}{8}$.

NUMBER & OPERATIONS - FRACTIONS EXTRA PRACTICE

1 Answer: C

Explanation: The number line is divided into sixths. One-sixth is identified by the point on this number line.

2 Answer: A

Explanation: 1 out of the 3 parts are shaded so the fraction that represents the shaded part is $\frac{1}{3}$.

3 Answer: B

Explanation: The shaded part of the picture is $\frac{1}{4}$. The fraction equivalent to $\frac{1}{4}$ is $\frac{3}{12}$.

4 Answer: D

Explanation: The number line is divided into 5 parts, and each part represents $\frac{1}{5}$.

5 Answer: B

Explanation: Equivalent fractions are generated by multiplying the original fraction by another fraction which is equal to 1. Equivalent fractions name the same number.

6 Answer: C

Explanation: 3 out of the 6 parts are shaded so the fraction that represents the shaded part is $\frac{3}{6}$.

7 Answer: D

Explanation: Equivalent fractions are generated by multiplying the original fraction by another fraction which is equal to 1. Equivalent fractions name the same number.

prepaze

8 Answer: B
Explanation: The fraction $\frac{4}{1}$ is equivalent to 4.

9 Answer: A
Explanation: The number line is divided into fourths. The bar represents $\frac{1}{4}$.

10 Answer: D
Explanation: The fraction $\frac{2}{8}$ is equivalent to $\frac{1}{4}$.

11 Answer: C
Explanation: The point on the number line represents $\frac{6}{8}$. This fraction is equivalent to $\frac{3}{4}$ and $\frac{9}{12}$.

12 Answer: A
Explanation: The number line is divided into 8 equal segments between 0 and 1. This number line represents eighths.

13 Answer: A
Explanation: The point on the number line represents $\frac{2}{8}$. This fraction is equivalent to $\frac{1}{4}$.

14 Answer: D
Explanation: Model A represents $\frac{1}{3}$ and Model B represents $\frac{1}{4}$. One-third is greater than $\frac{1}{4}$.

15 Answer: A
Explanation: Model A represents $\frac{2}{8}$ and Model B represents $\frac{4}{8}$.

16 Answer: C
Explanation: The model shows $\frac{8}{8}$ which is equivalent to $\frac{4}{4}$, or one whole.

17 Answer: D
Explanation: The distance between the park and Barack's school is the greater distance. ($\frac{4}{5}$ miles is greater than $\frac{3}{5}$ miles).

18 Answer: D
Explanation: The fraction $\frac{3}{1}$ is equivalent to 3 and $\frac{3}{3}$ is equivalent to 1.

19 Answer: C
Explanation: The fraction $\frac{3}{6}$ is equivalent to $\frac{1}{2}$, and is less than $\frac{6}{6}$ (or 1 whole).

20 Answer: $\frac{3}{1}$
Explanation: A fraction $\frac{a}{1}$ represents the whole number, a.

MEASUREMENT & DATA
UNIT 1: ESTIMATING MEASUREMENT & GRAPHS

1 Answer: D
Explanation: To find the hours, look before the : sign and to find the minutes look after the : sign.

2 Answer: C
Explanation: Flour is needed in the largest amount. 1 cup is larger than the other measurements.

3 Answer: D
Explanation: The hour hand points between the 6 and the 7. It shows 6 hours. Next, read the minutes. Start at the 12. Count by 5s until you reach the minute hand. The minute hand shows 19 minutes.

4 Answer: C
Explanation: Find Thursday then use the scale on the left side of the graph to read the value of the Thursday bar.

5 Answer: B
Explanation: The largest amount of cornbread is needed because 6 cups is the largest measurement out of the options.

6 Answer: A
Explanation: To find the hours, look before the : sign and to find the minutes look after the : sign.

7 Answer: D
Explanation: Find Clint then use the scale on the left side of the graph to read the value of the Clint bar.

8 Answer: B
Explanation: Find Friday then use the scale on the left side of the graph to read the value of the Friday bar.

9 Answer: B
Explanation: The hour hand points between 9 and 10, meaning it shows 9 hours. Next, read the minutes. Start at the 12. Count by 5s until you reach the minute hand. The minute hand shows 45 minutes.

10 Answer: D
Explanation: The smallest amount of garlic powder is needed because $\frac{1}{4}$ teaspoons is the smallest measurement out of the options.

11 Answer: A
Explanation: Since Lindsay must wake up in the morning to go to school, the time must be 7 A.M.

12 Answer: C
Explanation: Find the cheapest gas price then move to the right to find which state had the lowest.

13 Answer: B
Explanation: The unit gram is about the weight of a small paperclip, a toaster is heavier than 7 paper clips.

14 Answer:

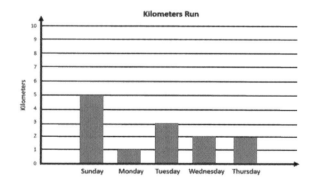

Explanation: Use the scale on the left side of the graph to read the value of each bar then fill in the correct value.

15 Answer:
Explanation: Use the scale on the left side of the graph to read the value of each bar then fill in the correct value.

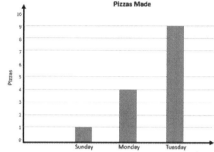

16 Answer: 4:00 A.M
Explanation: Look for a pattern. Each time is 1 hour later than the time before it.

17 Answer: A
Explanation: Grams would be far too small of a unit to use to measure a dog's weight with.

18 Answer: Fill in 1 book
Explanation: To find the table, 10 books must be represented in the December row. Coloring in 1 book represents 10 books, so 1 book must be colored in.

19 Answer: Scott ran a marathon
Explanation: Look on the timeline for 2013 and then look to see what is after it.

20 Answer: B
Explanation: A kilogram is too big of a unit to use to measure the weight of a muffin.

> ### MEASUREMENT & DATA
> ### UNIT 2: MEASURING LENGTH

1 Answer: A
Explanation: The line segment starts at 0 inches and ends at 2 inches on the ruler. The length is 2 inches.

2 Answer: D
Explanation: The line segment starts at 1 inch and ends at 5 inches on the ruler. The length is 4 inches.

3   Answer: B
Explanation: The line segment starts at 3 inches and ends at 6 inches on the ruler. The length is 3 inches.

4   Answer: D
Explanation: The line segment starts at 1 inch and ends at 6 inches on the ruler. The length is 5 inches.

5   Answer: A
Explanation: The sword starts at 0 inches and ends at 5 inches on the ruler. The length is 5 inches.

6   Answer: B
Explanation: The tulip starts at $1\frac{1}{2}$ inches and ends at 4 inches on the ruler. The length is $2\frac{1}{2}$ inches.

7   Answer: D
Explanation: The crown starts at 2 inches and ends at 4 inches on the ruler. The length is 2 inches.

8   Answer: B
Explanation: The dog starts at 0 inches and ends at 5 inches on the ruler. The length is 5 inches.

9   Answer: A
Explanation: The orca starts at 0 inches and ends at 4 inches on the ruler. The length is 4 inches.

10   Answer: B
Explanation: The car starts at 0 inches and ends at $5\frac{1}{2}$ inches on the ruler. The length is $5\frac{1}{2}$ inches.

11   Answer: A
Explanation: The candy cane is $2\frac{1}{2}$ inches long. One end starts at 2 inches and ends at $4\frac{1}{2}$ inches.

12   Answer: A
Explanation: The shoe starts at 0 inches and ends at $3\frac{1}{2}$ inches on the ruler. The length is $3\frac{1}{2}$ inches.

13   Answer: B
Explanation: The lizard starts at 3 inches and ends at $5\frac{1}{2}$ inches on the ruler. The length is $2\frac{1}{2}$ inches.

14   Answer: B
Explanation: The couch starts at 0 inches and ends at $3\frac{1}{2}$ inches on the ruler. The length is $3\frac{1}{2}$ inches.

15   Answer: $7\frac{3}{4}$ inches
Explanation: The crayon starts at 0 inches and ends at $7\frac{3}{4}$ inches on the ruler. The length is $7\frac{3}{4}$ inches.

16   Answer: $9\frac{3}{4}$ inches
Explanation: The candle starts at 0 inches and ends at $9\frac{3}{4}$ inches on the ruler. The length is $9\frac{3}{4}$ inches.

17   Answer: $6\frac{1}{2}$ inches
Explanation: The length of the lollipop extends from $1\frac{1}{2}$ to 8 inches on the ruler.

18   Answer: $6\frac{3}{4}$ inches
Explanation: The crab starts at 0 inches and ends at $6\frac{3}{4}$ inches on the ruler. The length is $6\frac{3}{4}$ inches.

19   Answer: $10\frac{1}{4}$ inches
Explanation: The length of the toaster extends from 1 to $11\frac{1}{4}$ inches on the ruler.

20   Answer: $3\frac{1}{2}$ inches
Explanation: The length of the gift box extends from $3\frac{1}{2}$ to 7 inches on the ruler.

MEASUREMENT & DATA
UNIT 3: AREA AND PERIMETER

1 Answer: B
Explanation: The area can be calculated by multiplying the length and width of the rectangle.

2 Answer: B
Explanation: Count the unit squares. There are 2-unit squares.

3 Answer: D
Explanation: Count the unit squares. There are 3 – unit squares.

4 Answer: C
Explanation: The perimeter can be found by adding the side lengths. 2(4+5) or 4 + 5 + 4 + 5.

5 Answer: A
Explanation: Count the unit squares. There are 4-unit squares.

6 Answer: C
Explanation: The perimeter of the figure can be determined by adding all side lengths.

7 Answer: C
Explanation: Count the unit squares. There are 12 – unit squares.

8 Answer: D
Explanation: The area can be calculated by multiplying the length and width of the rectangle.

9 Answer: C
Explanation: Count the unit squares. There are 12-unit squares.

10 Answer: B
Explanation: The perimeter of the figure can be determined by adding all side lengths.

11 Answer: D
Explanation: Count the unit squares. There are 6 – unit squares.

12 Answer: A
Explanation: Count the unit squares. There are 10-unit squares.

13 Answer: A
Explanation: There are 3 rows of 6 squares in the figure and one row of 3 squares.

14 Answer: B
Explanation: Count the unit squares. There are 6-unit squares, not 9-unit squares.

15 Answer: B
Explanation: The area of the blue figure is 23 square units. Each of the 4 rows does not have 7 squares.

16 Answer: Figure B
Explanation: The perimeter of the figure can be determined by adding all the side lengths. Figure A has a perimeter of 50 meters. Figure B has a perimeter of 54 meters.

17 Answer: 16 square units
Explanation: Count the unit squares. There are 16-unit squares.

18 Answer: A. 18 m
                B. Figure B
Explanation: To find the missing side of figure B, you must do 9 + 9. The perimeter of the figure can be determined by adding all the side lengths. Figure A has a perimeter of 32 meters. Figure B has a perimeter of 56 meters.

19 Answer: A
Explanation: The area of the figure is 19 square units. Each of the 3 rows does not have 8 squares.

20 Answer: 10 square units
Explanation: Count the unit squares. There are 10-unit squares, not 9-unit squares.

MEASUREMENT & DATA CHAPTER REVIEW

1 Answer: C
Explanation: Find the bar which is the shortest and then look down to see which day it is.

2 Answer: B
Explanation: A bottle of cough syrup is small, use milliliter.

3 Answer: C
Explanation: The line segment starts at 0 inches and ends at 6 inches on the ruler. The length is 6 inches.

4 Answer: D
Explanation: The number of square units in the shaded figure is 24. The area is 24 square units.

5 Answer: A
Explanation: Use the scale on the left side of the graph to read the valve of each bar. Then, add those valves.

6 Answer: C
Explanation: The area can be calculated by multiplying the length and width of the rectangle.

7 Answer: D
Explanation: The shaded figure has an area of 27 square centimeters

8 Answer: C
Explanation: The shorter hand is the hour hand. It points directly to the 6. The longer hand is the minute hand. It points to the space between 2 and 3 (approximately 13 minutes after 6).

9 Answer: D
Explanation: The perimeter of the figure can be determined by adding all the side lengths.

10 Answer: B
Explanation: The fish tank starts at 0 inches and ends at $5\frac{1}{2}$ inches on the ruler. The length is $5\frac{1}{2}$ inches.

11 Answer: B
Explanation: The perimeter of the figure can be determined by adding all the side lengths.

12 Answer: A
Explanation: Liters are used for volume a plastic grocery bag would hold more than a milliliter.

13 Answer: B
Explanation: The perimeter of the figure can be determined by adding all the side lengths.

14 Answer: C
Explanation: The area of the entire image is 100 square centimeters. The area of the shaded figure is 44 square centimeters. The difference is 56 square centimeters.

15 Answer: D
Explanation: Look at the shortest bar then go down to see which day it is.

16 Answer: D
Explanation: The area can be calculated by multiplying the length and width of the rectangle.

17 Answer: A
Explanation: The ice cream cone starts at 1 inches and ends at $5\frac{1}{2}$ inches on the ruler. The length is $4\frac{1}{2}$ inches.

18 Answer: A
Explanation: The shorter hand is the hour hand and longer hand is the minute hand. The hour hand is pointing to the 5, the minute hand points to the 3. It is 5:15

19 Answer: C
Explanation: The area of the third rectangle, Rectangle C, is the greatest.

20 Answer: B
Explanation: The number of shaded squares in the figure is 44. The figure has an area of 44 square units.

1 Answer: D
Explanation: The perimeter of the figure can be determined by adding all the side lengths.

2 Answer: A
Explanation: Liters are used for volume and a kitchen sink is heavy.

3 Answer: A
Explanation: The perimeter of the figure can be determined by adding all the side lengths.

4 Answer: A
Explanation: The duck starts at 0 inches and ends at 3 inches on the ruler. The length is 3 inches.

5 Answer: A
Explanation: To find the area of the purple shape, subtract the missing area from the area of the rectangle.

6 Answer: C
Explanation: Joshua would need 12 squares to fill the inside of the figure.

7 Answer: B
Explanation: Use the scale on the left side of the graph to read the valve of each bar. Then, combine those valves.

8 Answer: D
Explanation: The rectangle can be filled with 24 square units. The area is 24 square units.

9 Answer: C
Explanation: The shorter hand is the hour hand and longer hand is the minute hand. The hour hand is pointing to the 11, the minute hand points to the space between the 1 and 2 (approximately 9 minutes).

10 Answer: C
Explanation: Count the unit squares. There are 35-unit squares.

11 Answer: 12
Explanation: The area can be calculated by multiplying the length and width of the rectangle.

12 Answer: A
Explanation: A liter would be too large for a dose of cough syrup.

13 Answer: 41 square mm
Explanation: Split the figure into 2 rectangles and find the area of each then add up those 2 areas.

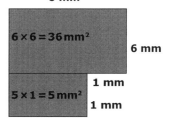

14 Answer: 18 square units
Explanation: The area can be calculated by multiplying the length and width of the rectangle.

15 Answer: 16 square units
Explanation: The area can be calculated by multiplying the length and width of the rectangle.

16 Answer: Answers may vary
Explanation: The library books were returned between 10:45 and 11 am.

17 Answer: 8 whole cookies
Explanation: Each whole cookie represents 2 batches. Alfonso made 16 batches.

18 Answer: Answers may vary
Explanation: Denzel watches a movie around 4:45 pm

19 Answer: B
Explanation: A car key is not very long so you would need to use the smaller of the 2 units.

20 Answer: The length and width are $7\frac{3}{4}$ inches and $5\frac{1}{2}$ inches

Explanation: The rulers on the edges of the rectangle show the length is $7\frac{3}{4}$ inches and the width is $5\frac{1}{2}$ inches.

GEOMETRY
UNIT 1: UNDERSTANDING SHAPES

1 Answer: B
Explanation: Two sides of a shape are parallel if lines placed along them never cross.

2 Answer: C
Explanation: Two sides of a shape are parallel if lines placed along them never cross.

3 Answer: D
Explanation: It has 4 equal sides but stands on a vertex.

4 Answer: A
Explanation: Two sides of a shape are parallel if lines placed along them never cross.

5 Answer: C
Explanation: All other shapes have one or more parallel sides.

6 Answer: D
Explanation: A trapezoid is a quadrilateral with one pair of parallel sides.

7 Answer: C
Explanation: Two sides of a shape are parallel if lines placed along them never cross.

8 Answer: B
Explanation: A trapezoid is a quadrilateral with one pair of parallel sides.

9 Answer: B, and D
Explanation: Rectangles have 2 opposite sides that are equal and parallel.

10 Answer: B
Explanation: They are all parallelograms. Each figure has a pair of parallel sides.

11 Answer: B
Explanation: This shape is a trapezoid. The top and bottom lines are parallel.

12 Answer: C
Explanation: The rectangle is a parallelogram.

13 Answer: A
Explanation: A quadrilateral is a polygon with four sides. So, square is a quadrilateral.

14 Answer: 4
Explanation: Vertex is a point where two straight lines or edges intersect. A quadrilateral has 4 vertices.

15 Answer: 1
Explanation: Two sides of a shape are parallel if lines placed along them never cross.

16 Answer: 0
Explanation: Two sides of a shape are parallel if lines placed along them never cross.

17 Answer: 3
Explanation: Two sides of a shape are parallel if lines placed along them never cross.

18 Answer: They both have the same number of sides and vertices. They are the same shape.
Explanation: The two polygons are the same shape. They are both pentagons.

19 Answer: Answers may vary
Explanation: A quadrilateral is a 4-sided figure.

20 Answer: Answers may vary
Explanation: A parallelogram is a four-sided figure whose opposite sides are

parallel. Square, Rectangle and Rhombus are examples for parallelograms.

GEOMETRY
UNIT 2: PARTITION SHAPES

1 Answer: A
Explanation: 1 out of 8 equal parts is shaded.

2 Answer: C
Explanation: 1 out of 6 equal parts is shaded.

3 Answer: A
Explanation: 1 out of 6 equal parts is shaded.

4 Answer: C
Explanation: 1 out of 3 equal parts is shaded.

5 Answer: D
Explanation: 1 out of 4 equal parts is shaded.

6 Answer: A
Explanation: 1 out of the 4 equal parts is shaded.

7 Answer: D
Explanation: 1 of the 3 equal parts is shaded.

8 Answer: B
Explanation: 1 out of 3 equal parts is shaded.

9 Answer: A
Explanation: 1 out of 2 equal parts is shaded.

10 Answer: C
Explanation: 1 out of 4 equal parts is shaded.

11 Answer: D
Explanation: 1 out of 8 equal parts is shaded.

12 Answer: B
Explanation: 1 out of 4 equal parts is shaded.

13 Answer: D
Explanation: 1 out of 4 equal parts is shaded.

14 Answer: B
Explanation: The first picture has fewer equal parts than the second picture, so the parts in the first picture are larger. More of the first picture is shaded.

15 Answer: $\frac{1}{3}$
Explanation: The model is divided into 3 equal areas. 1 shaded area represents $\frac{1}{3}$.

16 Answer: $\frac{1}{5}$
Explanation: The model is divided into 3 equal areas. 1 shaded area represents $\frac{1}{5}$.

17 Answer: $\frac{1}{2}$
Explanation: 1 out of 2 parts is shaded.

18 Answer: $\frac{1}{4}$
Explanation: 1 out of 4 parts is shaded.

19 Answer: Answers may vary
Explanation: The shaded part of this model represents 1 part out of 6 equally sized parts.

20 Answer: Answers may vary
Explanation: The shaded part of this model represents 1 part out of 8 equally sized parts.

GEOMETRY - CHAPTER REVIEW

1 Answer: B
Explanation: A rectangle has 4 right angles.

2 Answer: C
Explanation: There are 4 equally sized parts. One part represents $\frac{1}{4}$.

3 Answer: C
Explanation: A parallelogram can be defined as a 4-sided flat shape with straight sides where opposite sides are parallel.

4 Answer: D
Explanation: There are 8 equally sized parts. One part represents $\frac{1}{8}$.

5 Answer: B
Explanation: A rhombus is a parallelogram with opposite equal acute angles, opposite equal obtuse angles, and four equal sides.

6 Answer: A
Explanation: There are 4 equally sized parts. 3 parts are shaded.

7 Answer: B
Explanation: Each piece represents one-sixth of the pie.

8 Answer: C
Explanation: An object – the apple – divided into 2 equally sized parts means each part represents $\frac{1}{2}$.

9 Answer: A
Explanation: A kite is a quadrilateral with two distinct pairs of equal adjacent sides.

10 Answer: A
Explanation: A trapezoid is an isosceles trapezoid when both angles coming from a parallel side are equal, and the sides that aren't parallel are equal in length.

11 Answer: D
Explanation: The model is divided into 8 equal pieces. Each region represents one-eighth.

12 Answer: C
Explanation: A heptagon is a 7-sided polygon.

13 Answer: D
Explanation: There are 10 equal parts. 1 part is shaded.

14 Answer: D
Explanation: A rectangle is a quadrilateral with four right angles. A quadrilateral is a shape with four sides.

15 Answer: B
Explanation: There are 9 equal parts. 1 part is shaded.

16 Answer: A
Explanation: Count the sides of both shapes.

17 Answer: B
Explanation: There are 4 equal parts in the model. Each part represents one-fourth.

18 Answer: B and C
Explanation: Each figure had a pair of parallel sides.

19 Answer: A
Explanation: Two sides of a shape are parallel if lines placed along them never cross so there are none.

20 Answer: A
Explanation: The first model shows $\frac{1}{2}$. One half is greater than $\frac{1}{3}$.

GEOMETRY - EXTRA PRACTICE

1 Answer: B
Explanation: This model shows $\frac{1}{8}$. One-eighth is less than $\frac{1}{3}$.

2 Answer: C
Explanation: This model has 4 equal parts. Each part represents one-fourth.

3 Answer: B
Explanation: It has a pair of parallel sides.

4 Answer: B
Explanation: A trapezoid is a quadrilateral with one pair of parallel sides so II and III are trapezoids. A quadrilateral is a four-sided shape.

5 Answer: 2
Explanation: A rectangle has two pairs of parallel sides.

6 Answer: 6
Explanation: A model with a unit fraction of $\frac{1}{6}$ has 6 equal parts.

7 Answer: 2
Explanation: Shape A has 4 right angles. Shape B has 2 right angles.

8 Answer: Michael is incorrect.
Explanation: Two of the fractions are unit fractions ($\frac{1}{3}$ and $\frac{1}{4}$). The fraction $\frac{3}{4}$ is not a unit fraction. A unit fraction represents one part of a whole that has been divided into equal parts.

9 Answer: Jane is incorrect
Explanation: Every quadrilateral is not a parallelogram. A parallelogram is a quadrilateral with two pairs of parallel sides.

10 Answer:

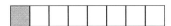

Explanation: The rectangle can be divided into 8 equal parts. The unit fraction is represented by shading 1 of the 8 equal parts.

11 Answer: $\frac{2}{6}$
Explanation: There are 6 equal size parts in the whole. Two shaded parts represents $\frac{2}{6}$.

12 Answer: Examples:

Explanation: A polygon with more than 4 sides could be a pentagon, hexagon, heptagon, octagon, nonagon, decagon, etc.

13 Answer: Trapezoid
Explanation: A trapezoid is a quadrilateral with only one pair of parallel sides.

14 Answer: $\frac{1}{6}$
Explanation: There are 6 equal parts. One of the parts is shaded.

15 Answer: The angles are both right angles. There are 4 angles.
Explanation: Students may give more than these descriptions, but common descriptions include: the angles in both polygons are right angles; there are 4 right angles in both shapes.

16 Answer:

Explanation: Both the rectangle and circle should be divided into 3 equal parts, with 1 part shaded.

17 Answer: Andrea is incorrect
Explanation: Not all quadrilaterals are a type of parallelogram. Not all squares.

18 Answer: Jalinda is incorrect
Explanation: The model does not have 2 equal parts. This is not a representation of $\frac{1}{2}$.

19 Answer:

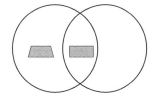

Explanation: A parallelogram is a four-sided shape with two pairs of parallel sides. A trapezoid has exactly one pair of parallel sides.

20 Answer: Isaiah is incorrect.
Explanation: More fractions can be modeled within this shape. For example,

prepaze

halves, thirds and fourths can be modeled. If each part has an equal area.

COMPREHENSIVE ASSESSMENTS
ASSESSMENT 1

1 Answer: A

Explanation: To solve $7 = n \div 3$ think of the related multiplication fact $3 \times 7 = 21$ and check the product using division: $21 \div 3 = 7$.

2 Answer: C

Explanation: The commutative property of multiplication states that two numbers can be multiplied in either order. There are 6 columns and 2 rows. So, you can multiply either 2 and 6 or 6 and 2 to find the answer.

3 Answer: A

Explanation: 3×4 is the equation used to solve because there are 3 groups of 4 apples in each group. Count 3 four times or multiply $3 \times 4 = 12$.

4 Answer: B

Explanation: The picture shows 5 groups of 7. If each square represents 7, 5 groups of 7 is the same as 5×7, which equals 35.

5 Answer: A

Explanation: Subtracting 10 ounces for the bag, the apples weigh 180 ounces, or 18 ounces each.

6 Answer: B

Explanation: The time shown on the clock is 4:16. The hour hand is on the 4, and the minute hand is past the 3.

7 Answer: B

Explanation: To find the minutes it took him to complete 5 circles, you can multiply 15 and 5. $15 \times 5 = 75$.

8 Answer: B

Explanation: The fraction $\frac{1}{5}$ is equivalent to $\frac{2}{10}$.

9 Answer: C

Explanation: The area of the shape is measured by unit squares with an area of 1 square unit. There are 13 square units in the shape.

10 Answer: D

Explanation: $9 \div 3 = 3$. The model shows 9 circles divided into 3 equal groups with 3 circles in each group. Think of the related multiplication fact to solve: $3 \text{ x} = 9$, $3 \times 3 = 9$.

11 Answer: C

Explanation: 5 times an even number will always result in an even number. When counting groups of 5, every even number of groups will end in a zero, which is even: 5, 10, 15, 20, 25, 30, 35, etc.

12 Answer: B

Explanation: $\frac{3}{4}$ is greater than $\frac{3}{5}$.

13 Answer: D

Explanation: Casey bought 3 s'mores for $4 each. Think of this as 3 groups of 4 or $3 \times 4 = 12$.

14 Answer: C

Explanation: Count the unit squares. There are 6-unit squares.

15 Answer: A

Explanation: Carla made 12 vanilla + 12 chocolates = 24 cupcakes in total. She can make 4 groups, each with 6 cupcake, because $24 \div 4 = 6$. Each will get 6 cupcakes.

16 Answer: B

Explanation: 56 biscuit is shared equally between 2 dogs. Each dog will get $56 \div 2 = 28$ biscuits. There are 7 days in a week. So, each day they will get $28 \div 7 = 4$ biscuits.

17 Answer: D

Explanation: The commutative property of multiplication states that two numbers can be multiplied in either order. There are 3 columns and 2 rows. You can multiply either 3 and 2 or 2 and 3 to find the answer.

18 Answer: C
Explanation: There is one shaded part out of three equal parts.

19 Answer: A
Explanation: The area of the rectangle can be determined by multiplying the length and width.

20 Answer: D
Explanation: The model shows 4 groups with 2 stars in each group. Count 2 stars 4 times or multiply 4×2.

21 Answer: C
Explanation: The perimeter of a rectangle can be found by adding the lengths.

22 Answer: A
Explanation: 10 beads on 6 necklaces means there are 60 beads total.

23 Answer: D
Explanation: The shape is a rhombus. All four sides are equal. Opposite angles are acute and obtuse.

24 Answer: D
Explanation: Four packages of 40 cups is 4×40, or 160 cups total.

25 Answer: D
Explanation: The number line shows fifths. The point marks $\frac{4}{5}$.

26 Answer: A
Explanation: $\frac{1}{2}$ cup is a larger quantity than $\frac{1}{3}$ cup.

27 Answer: 10-19 apples.
Explanation: Brea had about 40 apples, which means she has between 35 and 44 apples.

28 Answer: A
Explanation: The area of the rectangle can be determined by multiplying the length and width.

29 Answer: A
Explanation: The model shows 1 shaded part out of 8 equal parts.

30 Answer: Answers may vary. Total number of pages is 183.
Explanation: To find the number of pages Liam read, subtract the pages yet to read 111 from the total number of pages in the book, 238. Total pages Liam read is $238 - 111 = 127$. Similarly subtract 182 from 238 to find the pages Sophia read. $238 - 182 = 56$. Now add 127 and 56 to find the total number of pages they read. $127 + 56 = 183$ pages.

31 Answer: Sally is incorrect.
Explanation: The fraction $\frac{2}{8}$ is less than $\frac{3}{9}$. Sally assumed because the first column in both fraction models is shaded that the fractions are equivalent.

32 Answer: Answers may vary
Explanation: Answers may vary. The fraction $\frac{2}{6}$ is equivalent to $\frac{1}{3}, \frac{3}{9}, \frac{4}{12}$, etc.

33 Answer: Henrietta is incorrect.
Explanation: A model showing $\frac{1}{3}$ should have 3 equal parts with 1 part shaded.

34 Answer: Answers may vary
Explanation: Students should have 6 groups with 2 objects in each group.

35 Answer: 0
Explanation: The shape (triangle) does not have opposite sides.

36 Answer:

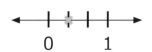

Explanation: The first hashmark after 0 represents the fraction $\frac{1}{3}$.

37   Answer: Brooke should have 4 signs colored in.

Explanation: Each symbol represents $10. Brooke had $40 and should be represented with 4 symbols in the picture graph.

38   Answer: $64

Explanation: Fist find the perimeter of the room since she want to border around the room. Perimeter can be found by add adding all 4 sides, $10 + 22 + 10 + 22 = 64$ feet. So, It would cost $64 \times \$1 = \$64$.

39   Answer: Answers may vary

Explanation: The equation $8 \times d = 48$ would help us find out how many days Irene did push-ups.

40   Answer: 4 square centimeters

Explanation: The area of a square (rectangle) can be determined by multiplying the side lengths.

41   Answer: Answers may vary

Explanation: 8×8 can help you solve 8×7 because if you know 8×8 is 64, then subtract a group of 8 $64 - 8 = 56$ to get the product of 8×7 because 7 groups of 8 is one less group of 8 than 8 groups of 8.

42   Answer: 7 jumps $7 \times 6 = 42$

Explanation: 7 jumps of 6 are needed to reach 42 because $7 \times 6 = 42$

43   Answer: Answers may vary

Explanation: In this case, each circle represents one whole. The whole is made up of only 1 part.

44   Answer: 12 square feet

Explanation: Using the outer blocks to measure the dimensions, students can determine the area of the playground.

45   Answer: 5 inches

Explanation: The envelope starts at $1\frac{1}{4}$ inches and ends at $6\frac{1}{4}$ inches on the ruler. The distance between each endpoint is 5 inches.

COMPREHENSIVE ASSESSMENTS
ASSESSMENT 2

1   Answer: C

Explanation: Since one pack has 4 toy cars, you would need to divide 36 by 4 to find the number of packs. $36 \div 4 = 9$ packs.

2   Answer: B

Explanation: The number line is divided into fifths. The point represents one–fifth.

3   Answer: D

Explanation: 3 rows + 2 rows = 5 rows; 5 rows $\times$ 5 equals 25.

4   Answer: B

Explanation: The model Wendy creates represents eighths. One–eighth was shaded.

5   Answer: B

Explanation: The keywords in this question are "leaving school". Kristen has practice in the afternoon.

6   Answer: A

Explanation: Counting by sixes to 54 is the same as counting groups of 6 to 54; $6 \times n = 54$ or $54 \div 6 = n$. $6 \times 9 = 54$ so Karl counted by sixes 9 times to get to 54 on the number line.

7   Answer: D

Explanation: The student recognizes $\frac{3}{5}$ and $\frac{6}{10}$ name the same number. This makes the fractions equivalent.

8   Answer: C

Explanation: $5 + 5 + 5$ shows adding five 3 times. Counting 5 3 times is the same as multiplying 3×5 because there are 3 groups of 5.

9   Answer: C

Explanation: If Samuel shares 4 cookies with 5 friends, think of this as 5 groups of 4 cookies. To find the total number of cookies Samuel had to share, multiply $4 \times 5 = 20$ or use the related

division fact: 20 cookies divided by 5 friends means they each get 4 cookies. $20 \div 5 = 4$.

10 Answer: A
Explanation: 24 cookies divided into 8 bags is $24 \div 8$, so to solve these using factors, think $8 \times 3 = 24$ because $24 \div 8 = 3$.

11 Answer: C
Explanation: First find number of minutes in 7 hrs by multiplying 60 and 7. $60 \times 7 = 420$. Now add the 45 minutes to find the answer. $420 + 45 = 465$.

12 Answer: A
Explanation: The shape is covered by squares which have an area of 1 square unit. There are 12 squares total.

13 Answer: B
Explanation: One–fourth is equivalent to $\frac{3}{12}$.

14 Answer: D
Explanation: $14 \times 3 = (9 \times 3) + (5 \times 3)$. 14 can split into $9 + 5$. Multiply each addend by 3, then add the product together. 14 is not being changes but split into addends that equal 14.

15 Answer: A
Explanation: 675 is 25 away from 700 and 75 away from 600. It is closer to 700.

16 Answer: C
Explanation: $\frac{5}{1}$ means dividing 5 into groups of 1. So, you will get 5 groups.

17 Answer: A
Explanation: $178 \approx 180, 63 \approx 60$ and $37 \approx 40$ so to estimate the amount of meals sold you must add $180 + 63 + 40$ which is about 280.

18 Answer: A
Explanation: $(45 - 3) \div 7 =$ First take the 45 slices and subtract the 3 she ate, $45 - 3$. Then divide the remaining slices by 7 $(45 - 3)$ must be completed first, then $\div 7$.

19 Answer: C
Explanation: The model shows $\frac{5}{8}$ shaded. Each part is represented by $\frac{1}{8}$.

20 Answer: D
Explanation: The figure can be covered without any gaps or overlaps by 15 unit squares which means the area of the shape is 15 square units.

21 Answer: B
Explanation: An eyedropper has a minimal capacity. Milliliters would be the best choice for describing volume.

22 Answer: C
Explanation: Demyan had $1\frac{1}{2}$ pumpkins in the graph. This represents $10 + 5$ or 15.

23 Answer: B
Explanation: 5 groups of 8 is the same as counting eight 5 times because there are 5 groups with 8 in each group: $8 + 8 + 8 + 8 + 8$, add 8 five times.

24 Answer: D
Explanation: $\frac{6}{10}$ is less than $\frac{7}{10}$.

25 Answer: B
Explanation: The number line is divided into thirds. The point represents $\frac{2}{3}$.

26 Answer: A
Explanation: The dimensions of the Art Center can be found by using the desks on the outside. The area of the Art Center can be found by adding $5 + 5 + 3 = 13$.

27 Answer: B
Explanation: The area of the rectangle can be determined by multiplying the length and width.

28 Answer: D
Explanation: Caleb has read 4 books because the table shows 4 books. Each book on the table represents 1 book.

prepaze

29   Answer: A

Explanation: The perimeter of the figure can be determined by adding the length of each side.

30   Answer: Answers may vary

Explanation: Students may start at 0, then "jump" to the right to 324. The next move would be jumping to the left 165 and 92 units.

31   Answer: $160

Explanation: The area of the room is 16 square feet and the cost per square foot of carpet is $10. $16 \times 10 = 160$.

32   Answer: Array should have 4 rows of 10 or 10 rows of 4

Explanation: The expression is equivalent to 4(10) or 40. This can be determined using the distributive property.

33   Answer: 8 teams

Explanation: To find the number of teams, first you must do 15+25=40 to find the total amount of children. Then you must do 40÷5=8 to find the number of teams needed.

34   Answer: A. $9 \times n = 54$
            B. $54 \div 9 = n$
            C. 6 chocolate chips in each cupcake

Explanation: 54 chocolate chips split evenly into 9 cupcakes means divide $54 \div 9 = 6$ or think 9 times what number = 54, $9 \times 6 = 54$.

35   Answer: $7\frac{3}{4}$ inches

Explanation: The hot dog starts at 0 and ends at $7\frac{3}{4}$ inches on the ruler.

36   Answer: 1

Explanation: The trapezoid has one pair of opposite parallel sides.

37   Answer: Answers may vary

Explanation: Students should have 4 groups with 5 objects in each group.

38   Answer: Zane is correct

Explanation: The model shows 5 equal parts. One part is shaded.

39   Answer: 36 square feet

Explanation: The area of a square can be determined by multiplying the length of one side by itself.

40   Answer: Even number

Explanation: An even number times an even number will always result in an even number because all even numbers are multiples of 2 so multiplying two even numbers $8 \times 4 = 32$ will result in an even number. The array made of 2 even numbers will be even: 8 rows of 4.

41   Answer: Answers may vary

Explanation: The value of n could be determined by creating a multiplication equation like $n \times 9 = 54$ or $9 \times n = 54$.

42   Answer: Bill is incorrect.

Explanation: $\frac{1}{3}$ is less than $\frac{5}{7}$. Since each shape represents the same whole, this can be determined by the amount of space (area) covered in each shape.

43   Answer: Arthur should work at the bookstore to make more money. $56 > $54

Explanation: If Arthur works 6 hours a week for $9 an hour at the coffee shop, he would make. At the bookstore, if he works 7 hours a week for $8 an hour, he would make $7 \times 8 = 56.

44   Answer: Oscar is incorrect

Explanation: The figure can be covered without any gaps or overlaps by 14 unit squares which means the area of the shape is 14 square units.

45   Answer: 2

Explanation: The parallelogram, by definition, has two pairs of opposite parallel sides.

Made in the USA
Columbia, SC
09 February 2021